# Mastering Crosstalk XVI

# Mastering Crosstalk® XVI

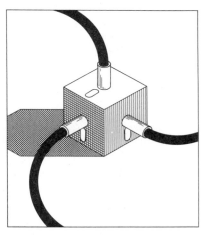

## Peter W. Gofton

San Francisco · Paris · Düsseldorf · London

Cover Design by Thomas Ingalls + Associates
Book Design by Jeffrey James Giese

*To Paula*

## Acknowledgments

I'd like to thank Chuck Ackerman and Dr. Rudolph Langer of SYBEX for letting me do this book, and my agent, Bill Gladstone, for arranging it. Thanks to Inmac for the photographs. Thanks to Paul Battaglia and Jan Bowers of CompuServe, Catherine Dille of The Source, and Carla Gaffney of Dow Jones News/Retrieval for access to their respective services, and to Stan Hayes and David Barksdale of DCA/Crosstalk. Any errors, of course, remain my responsibility.

I'd also like to thank my editor, Marilyn Smith; word processors, Dave Clark and Olivia Shinomoto; typesetter, Dawn Amsberry; proofreaders, Jon Strickland and Savitha Pichai; designer, Jeffrey Giese; technical reviewer, Saied Askary; and indexer, Jannie Dresser.

# Table of Contents

# Chapter 9: Transmitting Text Files     73

# Chapter 10: File-Transfer Protocols     81

# Chapter II: Terminal Emulation     93

# Part 4: Automating Crosstalk

## Chapter 12: Command Files

## Chapter 13: Script Files

# Part 5: Using Crosstalk with Information Services

# Introduction

Crosstalk XVI (referred to from now on as Crosstalk) is one of the most popular communications programs for the IBM PC. At the time of writing, it has an estimated 500,000 users.

Crosstalk is a powerful program, but many users do not take full advantage of its facilities. This book provides clear explanations of how to use both the basic and advanced features of Crosstalk.

Many people use Crosstalk to access on-line databases and other services. These services charge by the minute—more than a dollar a minute in some cases. Learning to make full use of Crosstalk's facilities can result in significant reductions in on-line time, and therefore in financial savings as well.

## What Crosstalk Does

Crosstalk is a program that enables an IBM PC or compatible computer to communicate serially, either through a direct connection to another device or by means of a modem. It obeys your commands, which you may enter from the keyboard or from a file saved on disk. Crosstalk can transmit text as you type it, as well as text that you've already entered and saved on disk. It receives data sent by a remote device, and can display the data on the screen or save it in a file.

Crosstalk can also send and receive nontext data, such as programs, and is capable of following several standard methods of encoding such binary data for transfer over communications lines.

Finally, Crosstalk can enable your PC to emulate one of several standard terminals.

## About This Book

I have tried in this book to cover the needs of both beginners and advanced users. Many people are already using Crosstalk, but they are not employing its more advanced facilities. The purpose of this book is to help both new and experienced users get more out of Crosstalk.

The book has been divided into five parts:

- Part 1 (Setting Up Your System) deals with installing Crosstalk and your communications hardware and setting up Crosstalk to be compatible with your particular computer and modem.

- Part 2 (Preparing for Data Transmission) covers setting the various communications parameters, dialing and disconnecting, answering calls, and customizing the keyboard.

- Part 3 (Sending and Receiving Data) covers capturing and transmitting text data, file transfers using protocols, and terminal emulation.

- Part 4 (Automating Crosstalk) deals with command files, script files, and facilities for programmers.

- Part 5 (Using Crosstalk with Information Services) gives examples of using Crosstalk with CompuServe, The Source, and Dow Jones News/Retrieval. Many of the techniques described in this part are applicable to other on-line services, so don't skip these chapters just because you don't happen to use those particular services.

## Crosstalk Versions

There are currently available three main versions of Crosstalk. The product simply known as *Crosstalk* is for CP/M computers. The version known as *Crosstalk XVI* is for IBM PC and compatible computers, and it is the version described in this book. *Crosstalk Mark 4* is an advanced communications program with approximately twice as many commands as Crosstalk XVI.

The latest version of Crosstalk at the time of writing was version 3.61. New releases come out from time to time, and future versions may add new commands, but the information in this book will most likely still apply to the newer programs. If you have a version earlier than 3.61, you may not have all the facilities described here, and you may want to obtain an updated program.

## Entering Commands

Each Crosstalk command can be entered in either uppercase or lowercase characters, and can be abbreviated to its first two letters. I have chosen to reproduce the commands in full in this book, for the sake of clarity, but you may come across sample Crosstalk command and script files that only use the first two letters of each command.

The key that you press to enter Crosstalk's command mode is known as the *Attention key*. This is generally the Esc key, but as you will see, you can change it to another key. In the instructions in this book, I have assumed that you are using Esc as the Attention key. If you are using a different key, then press that one when instructed to put Crosstalk into command mode.

## Sample Programs

The sample command and script files I have given, especially in Part 5, cannot be relied upon to remain usable, since the information services may change their command structures. The files should be regarded as examples of how to use Crosstalk, rather than as definitive usable programs.

# Part 1

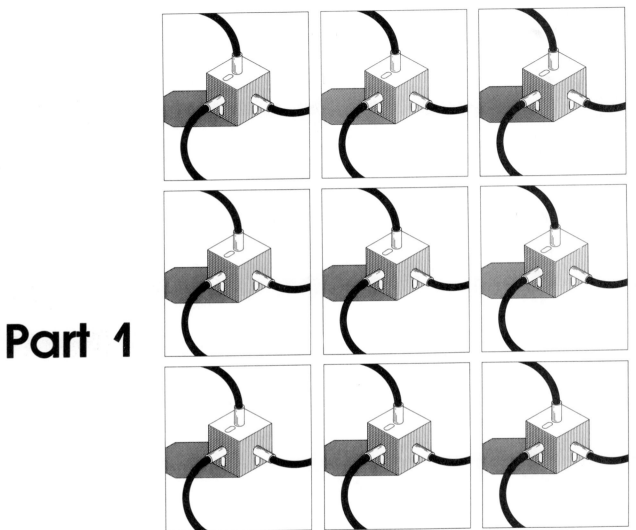

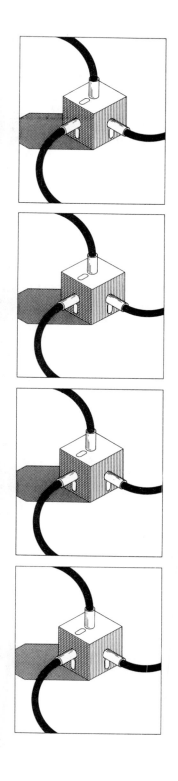

# Setting Up
# Your System

# 1

# Installing Crosstalk

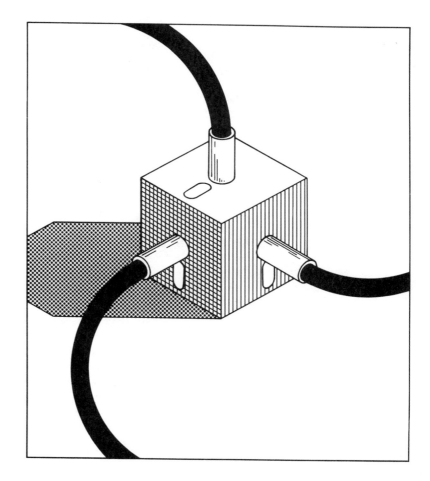

Before you can start using Crosstalk, you will have to install the program. If you haven't already set up your system, you may also have to install communications hardware. In this chapter, you'll learn how to prepare for loading and running Crosstalk.

# Installing Your Hardware

Crosstalk is designed for use with the IBM PC. There are several machines in the IBM PC series. There are also a large number of so-called *PC compatible* computers designed to run software written for the IBM PC. Unfortunately, some of these computers aren't so compatible in the area of communications. The expression *true compatible* is often used for computers that run all IBM PC software. If your computer is not a true compatible, it may not be able to run Crosstalk. Throughout this book, *PC* refers to all computers in the IBM PC series and true compatibles.

## Serial Interfaces

In order for your PC to communicate with another computer, you need a serial interface of some kind. The IBM PC does not have a serial interface built in, although many PC compatible computers do.

If your computer does not have a built-in serial interface, you need either a serial interface card or a multifunction card that incorporates a serial interface. (The enhanced IBM PC-AT comes with an adapter card that has both serial and parallel interfaces.) Alternatively, you could buy an internal modem, as discussed later in this chapter.

There are two main types of cards that provide asynchronous serial communications capability:

- Dedicated interface cards, such as the IBM Asynchronous Communications Adapter.

- Multifunction cards, such as the AST Six-Pack Plus, which incorporate a serial interface with other features. These function cards typically include one or two serial ports, a parallel port, a clock, and expansion memory.

Because there are a limited number of expansion slots in a PC (five on the PC, six on the PC-XT, and eight on the PC-AT), it is more efficient to use a multifunction card rather than a dedicated one.

**Setting Up Your Serial Interface** The IBM PC is designed to handle up to two serial devices, referred to as *COM1* and *COM2,* and you will have to set up your serial interface as either COM1 or COM2. Most serial interface cards have a switch for this purpose. If you have two serial interface cards, set one as COM1 and the other as COM2. Most software also can be set up to direct output to either COM1 or COM2.

In addition to setting up your card as COM1 or COM2, you may have to select the *IRQ* line. This is a circuit that carries the serial interface's interrupt signals, which notify your computer of certain events, such as the receipt of a new character. Each IRQ line in the IBM PC has a number. Normally, if your card is COM1, it will be assigned to IRQ4; if it is COM2, it will be assigned to IRQ3. You may find that the serial interface card has a jumper connection or a switch that allows you to choose which IRQ line the device will use.

Sometimes problems arise when two devices are trying to use the same IRQ line. For example, this happened to me when I had a mouse installed, which was using IRQ3, and then I installed a serial interface card that also used IRQ3. I solved the problem by changing the mouse to IRQ2, but I first had to make sure that no other device was using that line. I also had a problem involving a multifunction card that included a clock. The clock had been set up to generate an interrupt on IRQ3, also interfering with my serial interface card. Since I did not need the clock interrupt, I solved the problem by removing the multifunction card jumper that selected the IRQ line for the clock.

You can add more than two serial interfaces to a PC, but you'll need a special adapter. Before you buy such an adapter, make sure that it is compatible with Crosstalk.

**Connecting Your Serial Interface** Serial devices are generally connected by means of cables and *D-type* connectors (which are shaped something like the letter D). Each device, including your serial interface and any external modems or serial printers, has a D-type connector at the back. You need a cable, with a D-type connector at each end, to connect the devices together. Such a cable probably came with your modem. Some typical D-type connectors are shown in Figure 1.1.

## Modems

You can install either an external or internal modem. As far as your computer is concerned, an external modem is just another serial interface device, and you will need a dedicated serial interface card or a multifunction card to connect it to your computer. A typical external modem is shown in Figure 1.2.

**Figure 1.1:**

*D-type connectors. (photo courtesy of Inmac)*

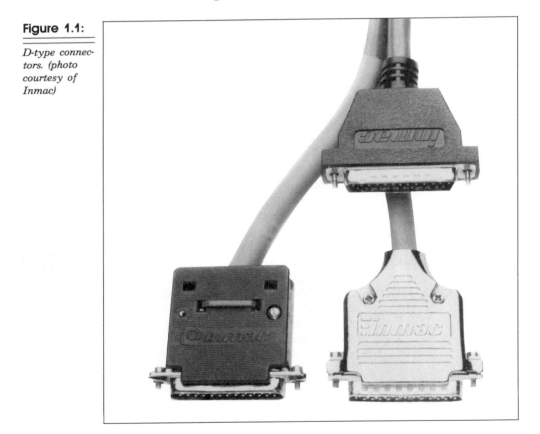

An internal modem, such as the Hayes Smartmodem 1200B, is contained on a card that is plugged directly into the computer. The computer sees it as a serial interface card, so that software does not need to know whether an internal or an external modem is in use. A typical internal modem is shown in Figure 1.3.

Internal modems are slightly cheaper than external ones, but they have two main disadvantages: they use one of the PC's few expansion slots, and they do not have status lights on the front panel. In addition, they are limited to use on one series of computers, which can be a problem if you ever want to use another type of computer.

## Installing Crosstalk

Before you start to use Crosstalk, you should make a working copy of the disk. Then store the original copy in a

**Figure 1.2:**

*An external modem. (photo courtesy of Inmac)*

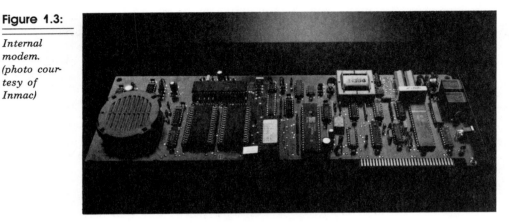

safe place so that you can copy it again if your working disk becomes damaged.

You can copy Crosstalk to either another floppy disk or to a hard disk. The program is not copy-protected.

Crosstalk comes with a number of files for accessing various popular communications services. You probably will not use all of these, but there is no harm in leaving them on your working disk until you are sure which ones you will need.

## Installing Crosstalk on a Floppy Disk

If you do not have a hard disk, you merely need to make a working copy of the Crosstalk master disk using the DOS DISKCOPY command. Follow these steps:

1. Place the DOS master disk in drive A.

2. Type

   DISKCOPY A: B:

3. When prompted to by DOS, remove the DOS disk and replace it with the Crosstalk master disk.

4. Place a blank disk, which will be your working disk, in drive B.

5. Press any key. DOS will copy the Crosstalk master disk onto the blank disk.

## Installing Crosstalk on a Hard Disk

If you are using a hard disk, you should create a Crosstalk directory for all your Crosstalk files. If your hard disk is set up as drive C, you can make a directory by placing the Crosstalk master disk in drive A and typing

```
C:
CD\
MKDIR XTALK
CD XTALK
COPY A:*.*/V
```

Now that you have a working copy, you're ready to load and run the program. After you get started, you will need to set some other configuration options within Crosstalk itself, as described in Chapter 3.

# 2

# Loading and Running
# Crosstalk

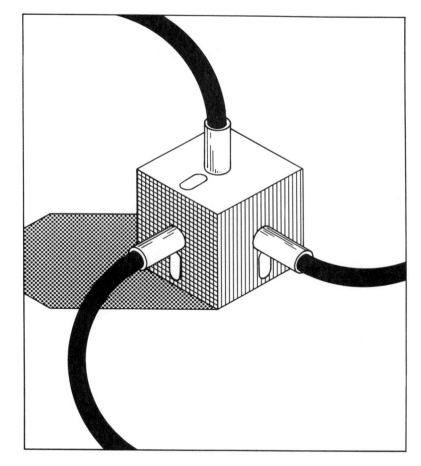

Now that you have installed your copy of Crosstalk, it is time to learn about how to load and run the program. This chapter describes how to use Crosstalk's principal commands and features.

## Loading Crosstalk

If you are loading Crosstalk on a floppy disk system, you only need to make sure that the Crosstalk working copy is in drive A and that the A> prompt is on the screen. Also, if you will be capturing data, then you should have a blank data disk handy. If you do not see the A> prompt, type

A:

followed by a carriage return. Then you can run Crosstalk by typing

XTALK

To load Crosstalk on a hard-disk system, first make sure that C (or whatever drive you've designated for your hard disk) is the current drive. If you do not see the C> prompt, type

C:

followed by a carriage return. Then make the Crosstalk directory the current directory by typing

CD\XTALK

followed by a carriage return. Then you can run Crosstalk by typing

XTALK

Once you've loaded Crosstalk, it will display a brief copyright notice, and then show the status screen. It will also execute any commands that have been saved in a special auto-load file (STD.XTK), which is described at the end of the chapter. When you first load the program, the display window (described in the next section) shows a menu of possible command files; these might be files for each of the different services that you regularly access or any other command files that you have set up.

# Screen Displays

Crosstalk displays two different screens. One of these, the *status screen*, shows the current settings for the program's principal parameters. The other, the *terminal screen*, shows the data currently being transmitted or received.

## The Status Screen

The status screen, shown in Figure 2.1, is the first screen that appears when you run Crosstalk. To redisplay the status screen later, you press the *Switch key*, which is the Home key (unless you define it as another key—see Chapter 7). Press the Switch key a second time to exit the status screen and redisplay whatever was on the screen before. You can also exit the status screen by pressing Esc in response to the command prompt, which is discussed in the next section.

The status screen displays the current settings of a number of Crosstalk's parameters. These parameters are discussed in detail in the next chapter and in Part 2.

**Figure 2.1:**

*The Crosstalk status screen.*

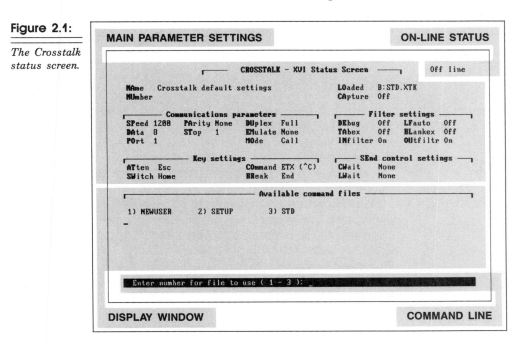

The status screen also shows whether or not your computer is on line. If it is on line to another computer via a modem, the words

On line

appear at the top right-hand corner of the screen. If it is in local mode (i.e., it is on line to a local computer or other device) the word

Local

appears. If it is not currently communicating with another device, you will see the words

Off line

Below the status information is a ten-line area called the *display window*. These lines are used for displaying additional information relevant to various Crosstalk commands. For example, if you enter the LIST command, Crosstalk will use this area to display more of the program's current settings.

At the bottom of the status screen is the command line. When Crosstalk is ready to accept commands from the user, you will see the command prompt, as discussed in the next section.

## The Terminal Screen

The other Crosstalk screen, called the *terminal screen*, is the one that you will probably want to see while your computer is communicating with another computer. It shows the last 24 lines of data sent or received. At the bottom of the screen will be one of two lines. If Crosstalk is in command mode, you will see the same command line that appears on the status screen. If Crosstalk is in on-line mode, you will see the *status line*, which gives you information about the communications session currently in progress. It tells you which keys are used for the Switch and Attention keys, whether you are currently capturing data to a file or to memory (see Chapter 8), and the time (in hours, minutes, and seconds) that you have been connected. As you will see, you do not need to switch to the status screen in order to give commands to Crosstalk.

Crosstalk automatically displays the terminal screen once communication with a remote computer has been established. Figure 2.2 shows a sample terminal screen in on-line mode.

## Entering Commands

You give instructions to Crosstalk by first entering *command mode,* and then typing commands from the keyboard. While the program is in command mode, it will interpret anything that you type as a command. When it is not in command mode, it will transmit anything that you enter from the keyboard to the remote computer.

To enter command mode, you press the *Attention key.* The Attention key is normally the Esc key. You can change it to another key using the procedure described in Chapter 7. Switching to the status screen also automatically places you in command mode.

**Figure 2.2:**

*A sample Crosstalk terminal screen in on-line mode.*

STATUS LINE ⟶

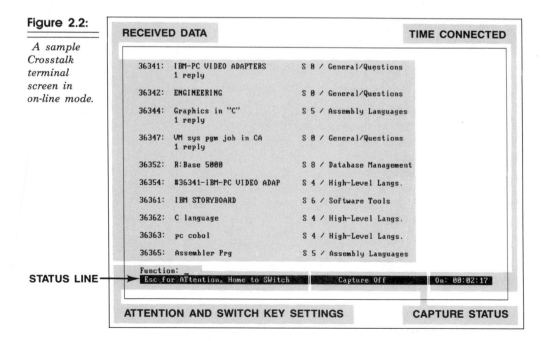

When you are in command mode, you will see the command line with the prompt

Command?

As you enter your commands, the words that you type will appear on the command line. Figure 2.3 shows a typical Crosstalk session in process, in command mode.

Most Crosstalk commands consist of two words: the command name followed by a parameter. For example, to set the telephone number to 123-4567, you would type

NUMBER 123-4567

The command name is NUMBER, and the parameter is 123-4567. Alternatively, you could abbreviate the command word to the first two letters, so you could enter something like

NU 123-4567

to set the telephone number.

A third way to enter commands is to type just the command name or its abbreviation, and then press the Enter

**Figure 2.3:**

*Crosstalk in command mode.*

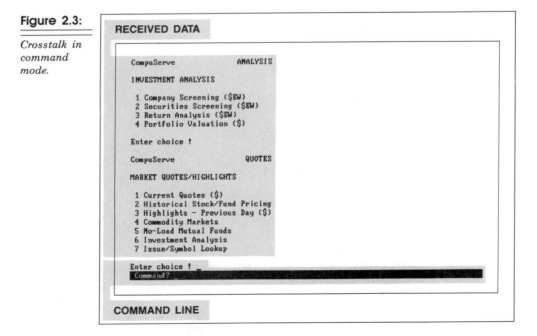

key. Crosstalk will then prompt you for the parameter. For example, you could enter

NUMBER

and Crosstalk would then prompt you with

Enter phone number:

You could then enter the telephone number, press Esc to cancel the command, or type a question mark (?). If you type a question mark, Crosstalk will give you a brief description of the command and its correct usage.

Another way to give Crosstalk commands is to create files on disk listing the commands. These are called command files and script files, and they are discussed in detail in Chapters 12 and 13.

## Common Commands

Some of the more commonly used Crosstalk commands are described below.

| | |
|---|---|
| HELP | Enables you to obtain help on a variety of Crosstalk functions. |
| PRINTER ON | Prints out everything currently being received or transmitted. |
| PRINTER OFF | Stops printing. |
| QUIT | Ends the current Crosstalk session and returns you to DOS. If you have any information in memory that you have not yet saved to disk (see Chapter 8), you will be warned and given a chance to save it. |
| XDOS | Enables you to leave Crosstalk without hanging up the telephone line. It is useful for some quick operations such as copying a file or referring to notes while in the middle of a |

communications session. (Remember that you may be being charged for the time while on-line, and that some remote systems automatically log you off after a certain period of silence.) Return to Crosstalk by using the XTALK command. You are already on line, and Crosstalk will not attempt to dial any numbers for you. Note that Crosstalk will be suspended while the XDOS command is in effect. If you want to be able to carry out another task while Crosstalk is working, you will need a concurrent operating system such as TopView.

RUN

Similar to XDOS except that you also enter the name of another program to run. Crosstalk is suspended while the other program is running, and it resumes automatically when the other program terminates.

EDIT

Enables you to run an editor or word-processing program. You must first tell Crosstalk the name of your editor program by setting the EPATH parameter. You also must be using DOS 2.0 or later and have sufficient memory for Crosstalk, any data currently held in memory, and your editor program. When you finish using the editor, you will be returned to Crosstalk. Using EDIT to invoke your favorite editor is an alternative to using the unsophisticated editing facilities offered by most on-line services.

# Directory and File-Handling Commands

Crosstalk has several commands that enable you to select a current drive and directory and perform some simple file-handling tasks. These are in addition to the commands for transmitting and receiving files discussed in later chapters.

## Displaying a Directory

Crosstalk's DIR command is similar to the DOS command of the same name. You can use it to display a list of the files in the current directory. To see a list of files on another drive, follow the command with the drive letter and a colon. For example

    DIR B:

displays the files in drive B.

Crosstalk's DIR command is more limited than the DOS equivalent; only the file names are displayed, only the current directory's files can be listed, and it does not display the names of subdirectories. You can use the /S option (described below) to get more information about the files, or change the current directory (described a little later) to see another directory's listing, but you will have to remember your directory structure if you want to access files in subdirectories.

Crosstalk has two additional options to the DIR command. The /S option (DIR/S) displays the sizes of the files. The /T option (DIR/T) displays the time, in seconds, that would be taken to transmit each file.

Unlike DOS, Crosstalk displays the file names in sorted order, and it needs to reserve memory space for this sorting. If you have a large number of files in the current directory, you may have to ask Crosstalk to increase the space reserved for sorting. To do this, enter

    DNAMES *X*

where *X* is the number of file names that will need sorting.

## Changing the Current Drive and Directory

You can use the DRIVE command to change the current drive within Crosstalk. For example, to change it to drive B, enter

DRIVE B

If you are using DOS 2.0 or later, you can create directories and subdirectories for your files, and you may sometimes want to change the current directory from within Crosstalk. The Crosstalk command for this is CD, just like the DOS command, and it is used in the same way. For example, if you have some files in a directory called WP, and you are currently in the root directory, you can enter

CD WP

to switch to that directory.

If you enter CD by itself, Crosstalk will tell you the name of the current directory.

## Deleting Files

You can delete a file from within Crosstalk by using the ERASE command. For example, to delete a file called BADFILE.DOC, enter

ERASE BADFILE.DOC

## Displaying Files

Crosstalk has a TYPE command similar to the DOS TYPE command. It displays the contents of a file on the screen. For example, to display a file called MYFILE.TXT, enter

TYPE MYFILE.TXT

If you enter this command while the status screen is displayed, the text will apppear in the bottom half of the screen, and you will be prompted to press Enter to display more text when that space is filled. If you enter this command from the terminal screen, the full screen will be used for the display, and the file will be shown continuously. Once you have initiated this command from either screen, you will not be able to switch to the other screen until you stop the display. To suspend the display, press Ctrl-S. To resume the display, press Ctrl-Q. To terminate the display in the middle, press Esc.

You can also display each line in a text file with the line number next to it. For example, to show the file MYFILE. TXT with line numbers, enter

TYPE #MYFILE.TXT

To display all lines in a text file starting from a given line, enter the line number after the command. For example, to display MYFILE.TXT from line 20 to the end, enter

TYPE 20 MYFILE.TXT

The last two options can be combined. For example, to display MYFILE.TXT from line 20 to the end with line numbers, enter

TYPE #20 MYFILE.TXT

## The Keyboard

As mentioned earlier, Crosstalk assigns special functions to the Switch and Attention keys. Functions of other keys and how to reassign them to new keys are discussed in Chapter 7. That chapter also describes how you can assign text strings or commands to the function keys.

# 3

# Recording Your
# Hardware Configuration

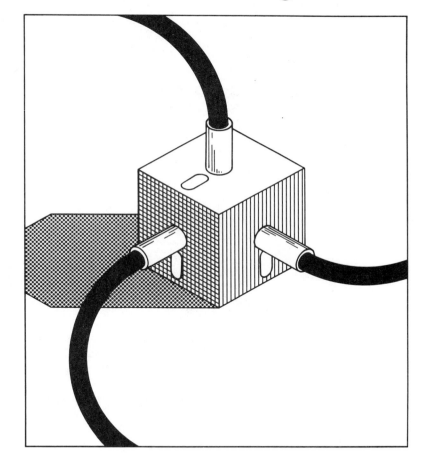

After you've loaded Crosstalk, you must tell it about the configuration of your computer system. You do this by setting various configuration parameters. Since the information probably won't change each time that you use the program, you can save it in a Crosstalk file that is automatically loaded. You'll learn how to do this at the end of the chapter.

Each of these parameters must be set in command mode. If you do not see the command prompt, press Esc before you begin.

## Communications Port

In Chapter 1, we discussed how a serial interface card must be set up as either COM1 or COM2. Now that you have Crosstalk loaded and running, you need to tell it which communications port to use. You do this by means of the PORT parameter. To tell Crosstalk to use COM1, type

    PORT 1

To use COM2, type

    PORT 2

## Type of Monitor

Your screen, or monitor, is attached to your PC by means of a display adapter. You must tell Crosstalk which type of adapter you have. You do this by using the VIDEO parameter.

If you have a color graphics adapter, enter

    VIDEO CGA

If you have a professional graphics adapter, enter

    VIDEO PGA

If you have an enhanced graphics adapter or any other type, enter

    VIDEO EGA/MONO

Note that it is the type of adapter, not screen, that is important. For example, if you have a color adapter with a monochrome screen, you should choose the color (CGA) setting. Otherwise you might get "snow" (white flecks or spots) on the screen.

Some PC compatible machines have the display adapter built in. In this case, the adapter is usually equivalent to a color graphics one, and you should use the CGA setting. If you have a problem with snow, it may be because you need to switch the VIDEO parameter to CGA.

## Screen Colors

If you have a color screen and adapter, you can use the SCREEN parameter to choose the colors displayed for normal and highlighted text, as well as the color used for the command line. You can specify the type of text, the foreground color, and the background color. If you only select one color, the foreground will be set to that color and the background will be black.

To specify the type of text, you enter its code:

| Text Type | Code |
|---|---|
| Normal | N |
| Highlighted | H |
| Command line and status line | L |

Follow the text type code with the color code or codes:

| Color | Code |
|---|---|
| Black | k or – |
| Blue | b |
| Cyan | c |
| Green | g |
| Magenta | m |

White        w

Yellow        y

For example, to set the normal text to white on black and the highlighted text to yellow on black, you would enter

```
SCREEN N w
SCREEN H y
```

You can also indicate the level of brightness for the foreground color; entering the color code in uppercase produces a brighter color than using lowercase. (Using uppercase for the background color causes the text to flash.) For example, to set the command line to bright blue on a red background, enter

```
SCREEN L Br
```

# Modem Parameters

If you have a Hayes-compatible modem, you will not need to set any of the modem parameters, since Crosstalk uses the Hayes parameters by default. If you have a non-compatible modem, you can refer to your modem's instructions and set the parameters yourself, or you can use Crosstalk's SETUP file (described in the next section) and choose a modem from those listed. If your modem is not on the list, you will have to set the parameters yourself as described below.

## The DPREFIX Parameter

Auto-dial modems require a special sequence of characters to be sent to them before the telephone number. Unless you tell Crosstalk otherwise, it will send the prefix ATV0E0X1 ¦ ˜ ATDT, which is the sequence sent to Hayes-compatible modems to reset certain default settings and to dial a number using Touch-Tones.

If you have a Hayes-compatible modem but do not have a Touch-Tone telephone, you need to change the end of this to ATDP. You do this by entering

```
DPREFIX ATV0E0X1 ¦ ˜ ATDP
```

Some non-Hayes-compatible modems do not use the ATD sequence at all. You can tell Crosstalk to send whatever prefix your modem requires. Just enter DPREFIX, followed by the characters.

You can include the following special characters as part of a prefix:

- A ¦ (vertical bar) places a carriage return at that point in the string.

- A ^ (circumflex) causes whatever character follows to be treated as a control character.

- A ˜ (tilde) tells Crosstalk to wait for 1 second at that point. Use one for each second that Crosstalk should wait.

## The DSUFFIX Parameter

The DSUFFIX parameter works in the same way as the DPREFIX parameter, except that it specifies a character sequence to be sent after the telephone number rather than before it. The following are some suffixes that work with Hayes-compatible modems:

- A ; (semicolon) means stay in command mode after dialing.

- An R means dial an originate-only modem (reverse the tones so that the answer tone is sent to the remote modem).

The default suffix is a carriage return, indicated by a vertical bar (¦).

## The APREFIX Parameter

If you want Crosstalk to receive calls from a remote computer, you need to tell it the sequence that it should send to your modem to put it in answer mode. Answering calls is fully described in Chapter 6, and you should refer to that chapter for information about how to set the APREFIX parameter.

## Saving the Configuration Parameters

You can avoid having to set the configuration parameters each time that you load Crosstalk by saving them in a file that is automatically loaded. To do this, set the parameters, and then enter

SAVE STD

This will create a command file, called STD.XTK, that is executed each time that you load Crosstalk. Unfortunately, SAVE does not record the color settings. If you want to record these, you will have to edit the STD.XTK file yourself using an editor or word-processing program.

An alternative way to save your configuration parameter settings is by using the SETUP.XTS command file supplied with Crosstalk. If you enter

DO SETUP

the SETUP file will prompt you for the type of modem and display adapter that you are using, and then create an appropriate STD.XTK file. However, it does not ask you for your choice of screen colors. If you want to choose your own colors, you should run the SETUP file first, and then edit the STD.XTK file.

## A Note About Defaults

There is an original STD.XTK file supplied on the master Crosstalk disk. Most likely, you will create your own STD file, as suggested in the previous section, or alter the original one by entering the settings that you will be using. These settings can include default communications parameters and function key assignments (see Chapters 4 and 7), as well as those for your hardware. Once you have altered that original STD.XTK file or created your own, your values become the default settings until you change them again. The status screen displays the current settings.

I do not refer to default values very often in this book because most users will create their own. However, when a default value is mentioned, I am referring to the setting contained in the original STD.TK file.

# Part 2

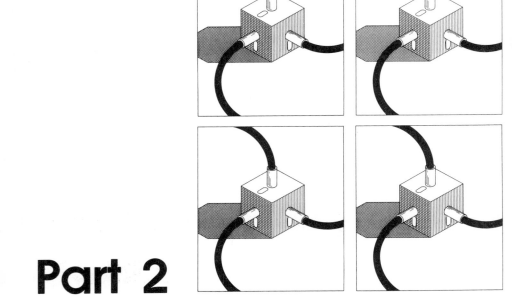
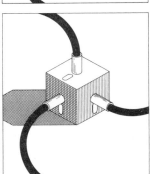
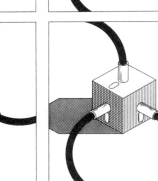
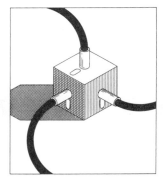
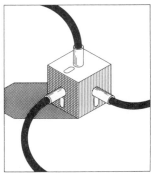

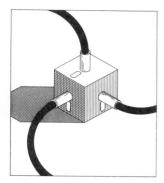

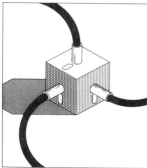

# Preparing for
# Data Transmission

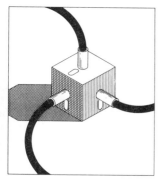

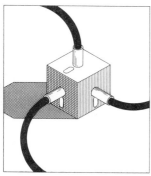

# 4

# Setting Communications Parameters

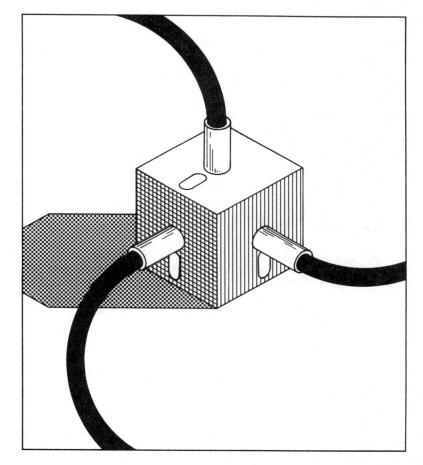

In the last chapter, you learned how to set certain parameters that are relatively fixed; they relate to your hardware configuration rather than to the requirements of a specific communications task. This chapter deals with parameters that are likely to vary depending on the particular task.

The most important parameters are baud rate, number of data bits, number of stop bits, and parity. The values to be set for each of these parameters will depend on the system with which you are communicating. For example, Compu-Serve requires 1 stop bit, a choice of baud rates, and either 8 data bits with no parity or 7 data bits with even parity.

All the parameters described in this chapter can be set either at the keyboard or through a command file (see Chapter 12). If you set them at the keyboard, you can then save them in a command file using the SAVE command. When you type in a communications parameter command, you can abbreviate it to its first two letters, just like any other Crosstalk command.

## Data Bits

Data bits are the bits used to represent each character transmitted. There will almost always be either 7 or 8 data bits.

The Crosstalk command for setting the number of data bits is DATA. For example, to set 7 data bits, type

    DATA 7

## Parity

A parity bit is a bit transmitted after the data bits to serve as an error-checking code. Crosstalk allows you to set the parity bit to even or odd, or to omit it.

*Even parity* means that the number of binary ones transmitted, together with the parity bit, adds up to an even number. Set even parity by typing

    PARITY E

*Odd parity* means that the number of binary ones transmitted plus the parity bit is an odd number. Set odd parity by typing

PARITY O

*No parity* means that no parity bit is sent. Set it by typing

PARITY N

## Stop Bits

Stop bits are bits transmitted to mark the end of each character. Crosstalk allows you to set the number of stop bits. Normally, 1 stop bit is used.

The command for setting the number of stop bits is STOP. For example, to set 2 stop bits, type

STOP 2

## Baud Rate

Baud rate is the speed at which the bits making up the data are transmitted. Sometimes you will see reference to bps (bits per second), which means almost the same thing, and the terms are used interchangeably here. The Crosstalk command for setting the baud rate or bps is SPEED.

Crosstalk offers a choice of eight speeds: 110 (entered as 0110), 300, 600, 1,200, 2,400, 4,800, 9,600, and 19,200. Most modems run at 300, 1,200, or 2,400 bps.

To set a baud rate, enter command mode and type SPEED, followed by the speed. For example, to set 1,200 bps, type

SPEED 1200

The rates can be abbreviated to the first digit in the number. For example, you could set 2,400 bps by typing

SPEED 2

Since 110 bps is entered as 0110, you would type 0 as the first digit. To set 19,200, you would have to type at least the first two digits (19), because it shares the first digit with 1,200.

## Flow Control

Imagine that you are on the telephone and you are writing down a name and address that someone is reading to you. You cannot write it down as fast as the other person is reading it. Therefore, you have to tell that person when to stop reading, so that you can record the information, and when to start again.

The same thing happens with computers. Sometimes data are sent faster than the receiving computer can deal with them. The receiving device has to send a signal to the sending device to tell it when to stop and start sending information. This is known as *flow control.*

The default characters that Crosstalk uses for flow control are Ctrl-S to stop and Ctrl-Q to continue. You can use the FLOW command to tell Crosstalk to use different characters. Enter

FLOW *ab cd*

where *a* is the character sent by the remote computer to stop Crosstalk from sending, *b* is the character used by the remote computer to tell Crosstalk to resume sending, and *c* and *d* are the characters used by Crosstalk to tell the remote computer to stop and resume transmissions, respectively.

To return to the default setting, type

FLOW SQ

To disable all flow control, type

FLOW −

## Break Length

A *break* is a special signal sent to interrupt the current operation of the system. It generally interrupts whatever program is running on the remote system and returns you to the operating system, or goes back to some earlier level of a menu hierarchy within a program. A break is useful for getting out of a program that has gotten into an endless loop or one that is offering alternatives that you don't want.

The break signal is a succession of binary ones transmitted for a longer time than it takes to transmit a regular character. Different systems require a break to be of different lengths. Crosstalk's default break length is 200 milliseconds. You can reset this length by means of the LBREAK command, followed by the length in milliseconds. For example, to set a break length of 300 milliseconds, enter

    LBREAK 300

## Line Feeds

When you reach the end of a line that you are typing, you normally want to continue at the beginning of the next line. This operation consists of two separate stages: the cursor goes to the beginning of the line, and then it moves down to the next line.

The ASCII code for a carriage return is 13. However, there is a lack of standardization among computer systems as to whether this should trigger the full operation (go to the start of the line and move down one line) or just trigger the first part. Systems that use a carriage return as only the first part send the ASCII code 10 for the line feed that moves the cursor to the same position on the next line. This is how Crosstalk operates.

Unfortunately, you may need to have your computer system communicate with one that disagrees on the meaning of a carriage return. If computer A sends a carriage return plus line feed, and computer B does the whole operation when it gets the carriage return, computer B will be going on two lines each time instead of one. If computer A sends only a carriage return, and computer B sees this as merely going to the beginning of the same line, all the lines will be typed on top of each other.

Crosstalk offers two commands to resolve this problem: LFAUTO and OUTFILTER. LFAUTO tells Crosstalk to add a line feed to each *received* carriage return. Use LFAUTO when the remote system is not sending line feeds after each carriage return. To use this command, enter

LFAUTO ON

To turn it off, enter

LFAUTO OFF

OUTFILTER tells Crosstalk not to send line feeds after each carriage return it is transmitting. To use it, enter

OUTFILTER ON

To turn OUTFILTER off, enter

OUTFILTER OFF

## Control Characters

Sometimes a remote system will send control characters that your computer does not recognize. The INFILTER command tells Crosstalk to discard all incoming control signals, as well as the eighth bit of all characters received. To turn on INFILTER, type

INFILTER ON

**Figure 4.1:**

*A sample Filter table.*

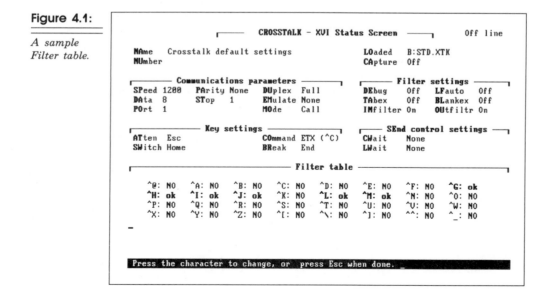

```
                    ┌──── CROSSTALK - XVI Status Screen ────┐        Off line

     NAme    Crosstalk default settings             LOaded    B:STD.XTK
     NUmber                                          CApture   Off

     ┌───── Communications parameters ─────┐   ┌───── Filter settings ─────┐
     SPeed 1200   PArity None   DUplex Full     DEbug    Off    LFauto   Off
     DAta  8      STop   1      EMulate None     TAbex    Off    BLankex  Off
     POrt  1                    MOde   Call      INfilter On     OUtfiltr On

     ┌────────── Key settings ──────────┐   ┌───── SEnd control settings ─────┐
     ATten  Esc                COmmand ETX (^C)   CWait    None
     SWitch Home               BReak   End        LWait    None

     ┌────────────────── Filter table ──────────────────┐
       ^@: NO   ^A: NO   ^B: NO   ^C: NO   ^D: NO   ^E: NO   ^F: NO   ^G: ok
       ^H: ok   ^I: ok   ^J: ok   ^K: NO   ^L: ok   ^M: ok   ^N: NO   ^O: NO
       ^P: NO   ^Q: NO   ^R: NO   ^S: NO   ^T: NO   ^U: NO   ^V: NO   ^W: NO
       ^X: NO   ^Y: NO   ^Z: NO   ^[: NO   ^\: NO   ^]: NO   ^^: NO   ^_: NO
     _

     Press the character to change, or  press Esc when done. _
```

To turn it off, type

INFILTER OFF

If your computer recognizes some, but not all, of the special characters being received, you can use the FILTER command to specify which control characters to allow and which to ignore. When you type

FILTER

Crosstalk will display a Filter table, which lists all the control characters. An ok next to a character means that it is allowed; a NO next to it means that it is not allowed. To change the setting of a control character, type that character, and the NO will change to ok or vice versa. Figure 4.1 shows a sample Filter table. To exit from the Filter table screen, press the Attention key (normally Esc).

After you have set the communications parameters required by the remote computer, you are ready to dial the telephone number that will connect you to it. The next chapter discusses dialing procedures.

# 5

# Dialing and Disconnecting

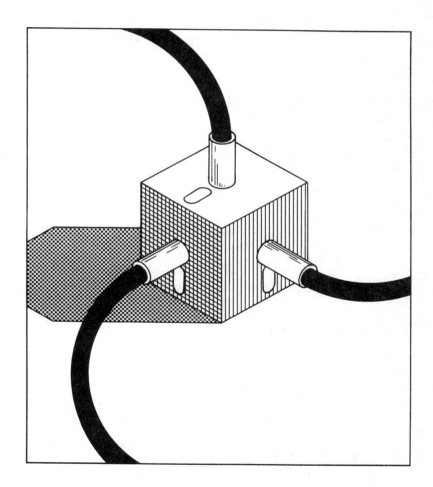

If you are using Crosstalk to communicate over the telephone system, you will need to be able to dial numbers. Crosstalk provides some dialing commands, and your modem may also offer some commands for controlling the call-making procedure.

This chapter explains how to dial a number and use the various Crosstalk and modem commands, as well as how to disconnect the line. The sample session at the end of the chapter gives you a chance to practice the procedure.

## Older Modems—Manual Dialing

Most early modems do not have an auto-dial feature, which means that you have to dial the number manually. If you have this type of modem, you will not be able to use Crosstalk's dialing commands—you still have to dial the number yourself.

After you have dialed the number and made the connection, enter

    GO LOCAL

and you will be in communication.

If you do not have an auto-dial modem, you can skip the following section. Note that if your modem is a Hayes or Hayes-compatible model, you can be sure that it has the auto-dial feature.

## Modem Modes

The following information applies to the Hayes Smart-modem, and it should also apply to Hayes-compatible modems if they are truly compatible.

The modem is always in one of two modes: command mode or on-line mode. While the modem is in command mode, your computer can give it instructions (through the serial interface between the computer and the modem). One such instruction from your computer to your modem is the command that tells it to dial a number.

Once connection is established with a remote modem, your modem will enter on-line mode. This means that it will no longer attempt to interpret any data that you send to it, so it will not accept commands from your computer.

Use the following settings when you are having your computer send commands to your modem:

- 7 data bits and 1 parity bit, or 8 data bits and no parity bit

- 1 stop bit, except at 110 bps, in which case there should be 2 stop bits

Most of the time, these settings will be compatible with those of the remote computer, but if they are not, you will have to change them after the connection is made.

## Dialing a Number

Having Crosstalk dial a number can be a simple process of entering the number and then telling Crosstalk to dial it, or it can involve complex parameters, such as waiting for a tone and transferring the call. To make a call, you use the NUMBER parameter and the GO command. Optionally, you can use the RDIAL parameter to tell Crosstalk how many times to dial the number when it cannot make an immediate connection.

Your modem may require a special character string to be sent before or after the actual telephone number. Special prefixes and suffixes are set through the DPREFIX and DSUFFIX parameters, respectively, as discussed in Chapter 3.

### The NUMBER Parameter and Dialing Commands

The NUMBER parameter simply tells Crosstalk to record a telephone number in its memory. A separate command (GO) tells Crosstalk to dial. For example, to tell Crosstalk to record the number 123-1234, simply enter

NUMBER 123-1234

After you enter a number, Crosstalk displays it just below the top left corner of the status screen.

Crosstalk treats the entry as a string of characters to be passed to the modem, rather than as an actual telephone number. This means that you can include in the string any special characters or commands that are recognized by your modem.

The following characters have special meanings to Hayes and Hayes-compatible modems:

| Character | Meaning |
|---|---|
| , | Pause (for example, while waiting for an outside line). The length of the pause is 2 seconds, but you can change it by specially programming your modem. |
| ! | Flash—the equivalent to holding down the switchhook button for ½ second. It can be used, for example, in transferring a call. |
| @ | Wait for one or more rings followed by 5 seconds of silence. |
| W | Wait for a second dial tone. |
| # | Give the tone for the # key. |
| * | Give the tone for the * key. |

Hayes modems ignore brackets, hyphens, and spaces, so you can add these characters to the number for clarity, but they aren't required.

The special characters enable you to set up quite complex dialing parameters. For example, the string

    NUMBER 9,123-4567,!#7127

means dial 9 for an outside line, pause 2 seconds, dial the number 123-4567, and transfer to another number (an extension). You could also dial an MCI or Sprint number, send a personal code, wait for a second dial tone, and dial a long distance number by using the form

    NUMBER 444-6666 , 12345 W 123-4567

Remember that NUMBER is a Crosstalk parameter, but the special symbols are commands to the modem. The examples above will not work if your modem is not Hayes compatible. Refer to your modem's documentation to see what other control commands you can use with it.

### The GO Command

Once you have told Crosstalk which number to use, you tell it to dial the number by using the GO command. Just enter

GO

Crosstalk will dial the number. If no connection is made, Crosstalk will display a message on the command line, offering to redial the number for you at selected intervals until it makes the connection.

You can tell Crosstalk how often to redial and how long to wait for a connection each time before giving up. To do this, enter the number of seconds between attempts, followed by a slash (/), followed by the number of seconds to wait for a connection. You can also have Crosstalk sound an alarm when it finally gets through by preceding the number of seconds with the letter R. Precede the seconds with the letter Q to tell Crosstalk not to sound an alarm.

The following example tells Crosstalk to dial every 20 seconds until it makes the connection, to wait 40 seconds for a connection each time, and to sound an alarm when it gets through:

GO R20/40

### The RDIAL Parameter

You can change Crosstalk's default setting for *how often* to dial using the GO command, but to change the setting for *how many times* to dial, you must use the RDIAL parameter. For example, to tell Crosstalk to try 15 times instead of the default 10 times, enter

RDIAL 15

## Hanging Up

When you have finished a particular communications session, it will be necessary for either Crosstalk or the remote computer to hang up the telephone. If the remote computer does this, Crosstalk will let you know that the carrier signal has been lost and return you to command mode.

If you want Crosstalk to hang up, enter the command

BYE

When you use the BYE command, Crosstalk lowers the voltage on the data terminal ready (DTR) line between your computer and the modem. Provided that your modem has been set up correctly, it will hang up as soon as the voltage on the DTR line is lowered.

The ATH command instructs a Hayes modem to hang up the telephone. However, it's easier to use Crosstalk's BYE command than to put the Hayes modem into command state and send ATH to it.

## A Sample Session

The following is a sample session that shows how you can use Crosstalk to dial a telephone number, make a connection, and hang up. In this example, you will enter the commands from the keyboard. In Chapter 12, you will learn how to incorporate them in a command file.

1. From the status screen, set the necessary communications parameters. For example, to set 1,200 baud, 8 data bits, and no parity, you would enter

   SPEED 1200
   DATA 8
   PARITY N

2. Enter the telephone number that you want to dial for practice. For example, to dial 123-1234, you would enter

   NUMBER 123-1234

3. Tell Crosstalk to dial the number by entering

   GO

4. Crosstalk sends to your modem the prefix character

sequence, followed by the sequence (1231234 in our example), followed by the suffix sequence. It displays

Dialing - 1231234 - Waiting for Connection - *x*

on the command line, where $x$ is the number of seconds left to wait (you will see the number reduced each second).

5. At this stage one of two things will happen.

   a. If the remote computer answers the call and sends a carrier signal to your modem, Crosstalk will go into terminal mode and display the terminal screen. From then on, anything you type will be transmitted to the remote computer and anything received from the remote computer will be displayed on the screen.

   b. If Crosstalk does not make a connection with the remote computer (the line is busy or the remote computer does not answer), Crosstalk will display the message

      No answer. Would you like to redial periodically (Y/N)?

      If you enter N, you will be returned to the regular command prompt. If you enter Y, you will be asked

      Re-dial how often (in seconds)?

      You can enter a number of seconds here. If you simply press Return, Crosstalk will abandon the attempt to get through and display the command prompt. Otherwise, it will redial the number every $x$ seconds, where $x$ is the number that you entered. The number of attempts it makes will be the number currently set under the RDIAL parameter (the default is 10).

6. When you have finished your call, one of two things will happen.

   a. If the remote computer hangs up the telephone at the end of the communications session, Crosstalk will return to command mode and show the prompt

Carrier lost. press ENTER:

This message is not an indication of a naval disaster. The carrier is the tone sent by the remote computer while a communications session is in progress, and your modem notifies Crosstalk when this tone disappears by lowering the voltage on the carrier-detect line between the modem and your computer. When you see this message, press Return. Crosstalk will display the regular command prompt.

b. If it is up to you to hang up the telephone, enter command mode by pressing the Attention key (normally Esc), and type

BYE

This causes Crosstalk to lower the voltage on the DTR line to your modem, and your modem will hang up the telephone. Crosstalk will then display the command prompt.

In the next chapter, you will learn how to customize the keyboard. Then you will be ready to send and receive data.

# 6

# Answering Calls

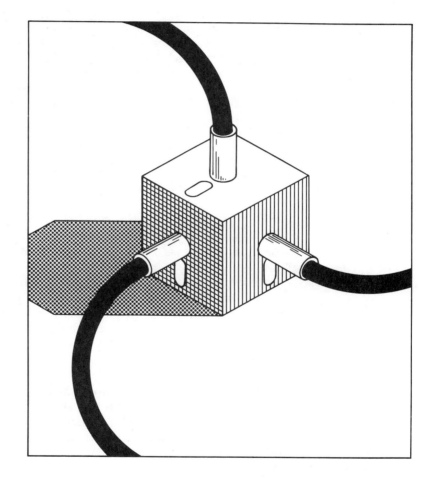

Although you may only have considered using the program to initiate calls, Crosstalk can also be used to answer calls received from a remote computer. This chapter explains how to set Crosstalk and your modem in answer mode. It also describes how to set up a password system, transmit a greeting message, and control the level of the remote user's access.

It is not necessary for the other computer to be running Crosstalk, and the other computer does not even have to be a PC. I tested out the examples given in this chapter by using a UNIX-based minicomputer to call my PC.

## Entering Answer Mode

Crosstalk and your modem must be in answer mode to receive calls rather than originate them. In order to enter answer mode, Crosstalk must instruct your modem to answer the phone. If you have a Hayes-compatible modem, the command string that puts the modem in answer mode is

    ATS0 = X

where $X$ is the number of rings to wait before answering. (Note that if $X$ is zero, the modem will not answer the call at all.)

You use the APREFIX parameter to tell Crosstalk what command string to send to the modem to put it in answer mode. For example, to tell Crosstalk to set a Hayes-compatible modem to answer on the third ring, you would enter

    APREFIX ATS0 = 3|

The vertical bar (|) indicates a carriage return, which Crosstalk must send at the end of the string.

If you have another type of modem, refer to its documentation for the command to put it in answer mode.

Setting the APREFIX parameter does not put the modem or program into answer mode; it simply tells Crosstalk what string to send to the modem. You put Crosstalk into answer mode by entering the commands

    MODE ANSWER
    GO

Crosstalk will then send the command string that you entered with the APREFIX parameter to the modem, and they will both be in answer mode.

When Crosstalk is in answer mode, it will obey most commands coming from the remote system. Characters sent to the remote modem will be echoed on the screen, and characters received from the remote modem will be echoed back to it.

## Cancelling Answer Mode

To tell Crosstalk to cancel answer mode, you would enter

MODE CALL

This does not actually tell the modem not to answer the telephone. Instead, it tells Crosstalk to lower the voltage on the DTR line to the modem. If the modem is properly set up, it will not answer the telephone when DTR is low.

If you want to tell the modem itself not to answer the telephone, you have to send it the appropriate command manually. To communicate with the modem from the keyboard, issue the command

GO LOCAL

Then type the command not to answer the phone. For a Hayes-compatible modem, this command is

ATS0 = 0

Exit local mode by entering

BYE

## Receiving a Call

When a call is received, the modem will answer the telephone and indicate to Crosstalk that a call is coming in. What happens next depends on what you've programmed Crosstalk to do. You can set up a password system to screen callers, transmit a greeting message, and set the level of the remote user's access.

## Passwords

You can program Crosstalk to require the remote system to enter a password. To do this, enter the PWORD command, followed by the password. For example, to use the password SECRET (not a very good one, by the way), before you put the system in answer mode, enter

PWORD SECRET

When Crosstalk receives a call, it will transmit to the remote computer's screen the message

Enter Password:

followed by a Ctrl-E code. If the remote system is also using Crosstalk, it can be programmed (using the ANS-BACK command) to transmit a particular string when the Ctrl-E character is received. For example, the remote user could give his or her system the command

ANSBACK SECRET|

and it would automatically send the correct password.

Crosstalk will then wait for the remote system to transmit the correct password. If it doesn't receive the password, Crosstalk will display the message and wait for the correct response two more times before hanging up the telephone and waiting for another call.

## Greeting Messages

Once a valid password (if any) has been received, Crosstalk can transmit your greeting message. You enter the text for a greeting using the NAME command. For example, to instruct Crosstalk to send the message *Welcome to Peter's PC System*, you would enter

NAME Welcome to Peter's PC System|

The vertical bar, which represents a carriage return, is included to place the cursor on the next line after the message is received.

## Remote Commands

At this stage, Crosstalk will wait for the *command character* to be received from the remote system. The command character is normally Ctrl-C, but you can change it to something else by using the COMMAND command. For example, to change it to Ctrl-D, enter

COMMAND ^D

When Crosstalk receives this character (normally typed by the user at the other end, but sometimes transmitted by a script file—see Chapter 12), it sends a string requesting the remote user to enter a command. Crosstalk is set to display

Command?

but you can change it by placing an alternative string in the Shift-F4 function-key combination, as described in Chapter 7.

From then on, the remote user can enter many of the normal Crosstalk commands, and Crosstalk will respond as if they had been typed locally. However, for your protection, some commands (such as ERASE and QUIT) will not be accepted. Some other commands will be effective only if you have told Crosstalk to accept them. This is done by using the ACCEPT command.

There are four levels of access that can be set by the ACCEPT command:

| Command | Access Level |
|---|---|
| ACCEPT Everything | Allows most of the Crosstalk commands to be accepted. |
| ACCEPT Nothing | Allows files to be transmitted to the remote system, but not to be received or altered. |
| ACCEPT Appends | Allows data to be appended to the end of existing local files, but does not allow new files to be created. |
| ACCEPT Creates | Allows data to be appended and new files to be created, but does not allow existing files to be overwritten. |

## Advanced Uses of Remote Commands

If you set the level of access using ACCEPT Everything, the remote user can send the command QUIT, in which case

Crosstalk will not answer any more calls.

In addition, the remote user can send the command XDOS, which terminates Crosstalk without hanging up. This capability can be used for some advanced programming. For example, imagine that Crosstalk had been running under a batch file that read

```
XTALK MYSCRIPT
APROG
XTALK MYSCRIPT
```

When the remote user sent in the command XDOS, Crosstalk would terminate, and the next command in the batch file (APROG) would be run. The APROG program would be executed, and then Crosstalk would be invoked again. APROG could be a program that reads a data file that was created during the first Crosstalk session, uses these data to produce a report, and saves the report in another file. During the second Crosstalk session, the remote user could read the report file and see the results.

There are many practical applications for such use of remote commands. For example, the computer at a company's headquarters could be programmed to dial each branch every night and obtain the day's closing figures.

# 7

# Customizing the Keyboard

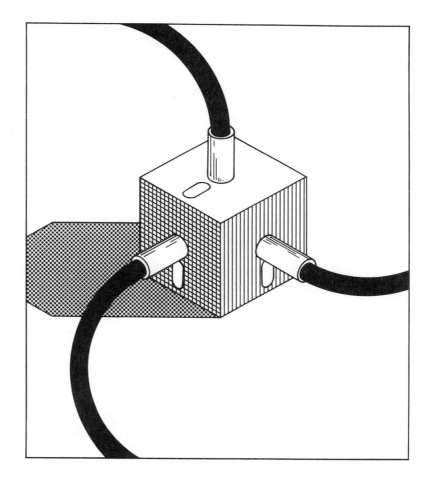

Crosstalk offers you quite a bit of flexibility in defining the functions of keys on the keyboard. As you've learned in earlier chapters, Crosstalk has assigned special meanings to certain keys. If you want to, you can reassign these meanings to any other keys that do not display a character on the screen (for example, Ctrl-D). Furthermore, you can assign text and commands to all the function keys and function-key combinations. In this chapter, you'll learn how to change the special keys and assign text strings or commands to the function keys.

## The Attention Key

The Attention key is the key that you press to switch from on-line to command mode. When you first load Crosstalk, the Attention key is the Esc key. However, the Esc key represents a valid ASCII character (number 27), and you may have to communicate with a remote computer that asks you to press this key. Since you would not want Crosstalk to intercept this signal and put you in command mode instead of sending the Escape character to the remote system, you may want to change the Attention key to another key.

To tell Crosstalk to use another key (one that does not display a character) as the Attention key, use the ATTENTION command. There are four ways of using the command:

- Enter the ATTENTION command by itself, and Crosstalk will ask you to press the key to be used as the Attention key.

- Enter the ATTENTION command followed by the name of the key. For Ctrl-A through Ctrl-Z, use a circumflex before the letter (e.g., ^C for Ctrl-C). For the Home, PgUp, End, and PgDn keys, type their names (e.g., ATTENTION PgDn).

- Enter the ATTENTION command followed by the ASCII code (in hexadecimal arithmetic) of the key that you want to use instead.

- Enter the ATTENTION command followed by the ASCII mnemonic for the key. The mnemonics for each

Ctrl-key combination character (for example, EOT for Ctrl-D) are listed on the ASCII table.

The first method is the easiest. The others are more appropriate for use in command files, which are described in Chapter 12.

## The Break Key

As discussed in Chapter 4, the break signal is a special signal sent to a remote computer. It often has a similar effect to pressing Ctrl-C on a microcomputer; that is, it generally interrupts execution of the current program and returns you to the operating system or to a higher level function.

The Break key is normally the End key on the numeric keypad. However, Crosstalk offers a BREAK command, which enables you to tell Crosstalk which key you intend to press when you want to send a break signal. The BREAK command works in the same way as the ATTENTION command: you can enter the command alone and have Crosstalk prompt you for the replacement key, follow the command by the ASCII code for the key, or follow it by the ASCII mnemonic for the key.

## The Switch Key

The Switch key displays Crosstalk's status screen and is normally the Home key on your keyboard. You can assign it to another key by using the SWITCH command. The SWITCH command works the same way as the ATTENTION and BREAK commands.

## The Enter Key

Many computer terminals have separate Enter and Return keys. They can have different meanings, depending on the software in use. If you will be transmitting data to a system that uses a different code for Enter, you may want to change the one that Crosstalk sends.

To instruct Crosstalk to send a different code when you press Enter, use the TURNAROUND command. Just as with the other key reassignment commands, you can simply type in TURNAROUND and wait for Crosstalk to ask you to press the key that represents the code that you want to be sent each time that the Enter key is pressed, or you can enter the ASCII number or mnemonic for the character that you want to send.

## Function Keys

You can assign any string of characters to any function key (F1 through F10) or function-key combination by the use of the FKEYS command. The string can be text that you want to insert or commands that you want initiated when your press the key.

The STD.XTK command file supplied with Crosstalk contains the following preset function key assignments. You can change these by editing the STD.XTK file or by using the FKEYS command, as described below.

| Key | String | Function |
| --- | --- | --- |
| F4 | CROSSTALK—XVI | Contains the name of the program. |
| F5 | @CApture /¦ | Toggles the capture function on and off. |
| F6 | @PRinter /¦ | Toggles the printer on and off. |
| F7 | @TYpe ¦ | Displays the contents of the capture buffer. |
| F8 | @CApture <24¦ | Places the last 24 lines in the capture buffer. |
| F9 | @SNap ¦ | Displays the snapshot buffer. |
| F10 | @SNap 24¦ | Saves the screen in the snapshot buffer. |

The CAPTURE and SNAPSHOT commands are explained in Chapter 8.

## Assigning Text

Assigning text to a function key can save a lot of time if you have certain phrases that you use repeatedly. For example, if you usually end your electronic mail with the same closing and your name, you could avoid having to keep typing these same words by assigning them to a function key. I assigned my closing to F3 as follows:

FKEYS 3 Best wishes ... Peter¦

You are not limited to the ten function keys F1 through F10. You can assign strings to the Alt-, Shift-, and Ctrl-function key combinations—you actually have 40 keys to use as you please!

To assign a string to an Alt-key combination, precede the function key number with the letter A. For example, you could assign a letter closing to the Alt-F10 combination by entering

FKEYS A10 Yours truly¦Mary Jones¦

In this example, the vertical bar characters (¦) cause Crosstalk to transmit a carriage return at those points in the string. Crosstalk would actually send

Yours truly
Mary Jones

when you press Alt-F10.

To assign a string to a Shift-key combination, precede the function key number with the letter S. For example, to assign the company name Communications, Inc. to Shift-F3, you would enter

FKEYS S3 Communications, Inc.

In Chapter 6, we saw that the command prompt sent to a remote system when Crosstalk is in answer mode is stored in Shift-F4. To change it to *What shall I do next?*, enter

FKEYS S4 What shall I do next?¦

You can assign a string to a Ctrl-key combination by preceding the function key number with the letter C. For example, to assign the phrase *Please respond promptly.* to Ctrl-F4, enter

FKEYS C4 Please respond promptly.

## Assigning Commands

You can also use the function keys and function-key combinations to hold strings that are commands to Crosstalk. If you want Crosstalk actually to perform the operation rather than insert the stored text, precede the stored string with an at sign (@). Suppose, for example, that you have several different telephone numbers that you want Crosstalk to dial. You could assign each number and the GO command to a function key, like this:

FKEYS C2 @NU 123-1234¦GO¦
FKEYS C3 @NU 123-1235¦GO¦

Then all you have to do to have Crosstalk dial the first number is press Ctrl-F2. Press Ctrl-F3 to have it dial the second number. If the dialing procedure involves waiting for a dial tone or another type of pause, you can use the tilde symbol (˜) to instruct Crosstalk to pause for 2 seconds at that point.

## Viewing Function Key Assignments

You can also use the FKEYS command to display the current function key assignments. To see the text or commands assigned to the regular function keys, enter the FKEYS command by itself. Display the Shift-function key assignments by entering

FKEYS S

Similarly, following the command with an A shows the Alt-function key assignments, and following it with a C displays the Ctrl-function key assignments.

Assigning the text strings and commands that you use often to function keys will help you to prepare for the main task: sending or receiving data. The next chapters discuss the details of data transmission.

# Part 3

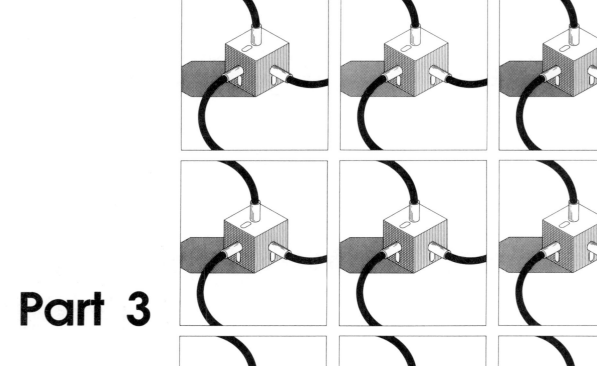
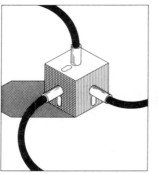
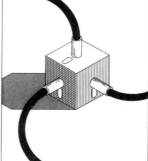
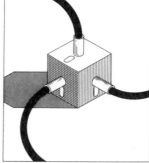
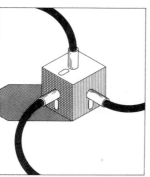
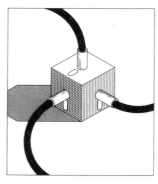
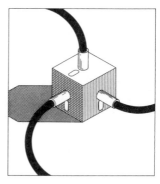

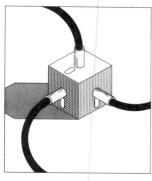

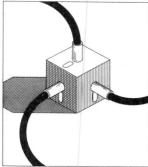

# Sending and Receiving Data

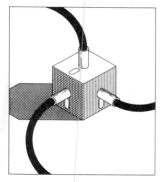

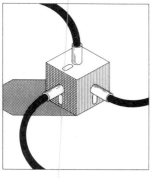

# 8

# Capturing Text Files

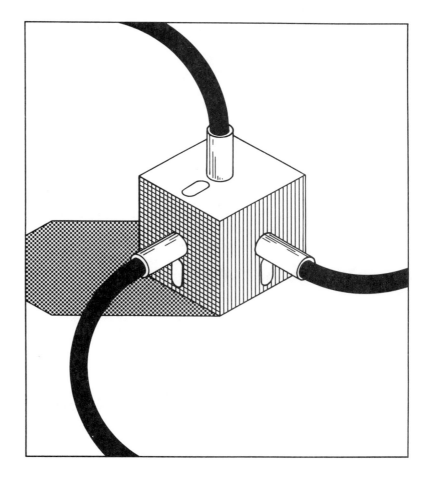

Imagine that you have successfully used Crosstalk to dial an on-line database, and you are finding all sorts of useful information. The information is being displayed on your screen line by line. Once the screen is full, the older information starts scrolling off the top of the screen and disappearing into the electronic void. In this chapter, you'll learn how to capture that information before it is lost.

This chapter deals with the transfer of regular text files. If you want to receive nontext data, such as programs or spreadsheet files, you will have to use a special communications protocol, as discussed in Chapter 9. Some word-processing programs save text in nonstandard format, and these files also may have to be transferred using a communications protocol.

# Transferring Data to Memory

You can instruct Crosstalk to copy, or *capture,* all information into your computer's memory as it is received or transmitted. The area of memory in which these data are saved is known as a *capture buffer.*

## Using the CAPTURE Command

Crosstalk does not automatically copy information into memory. You must use the CAPTURE command to turn the capture buffer on. When you want to begin capturing data, type

CAPTURE +

Crosstalk will tell you, by a message on the status line, how much memory you have available as follows:

Capture On, xxxK free

You will see this amount decrease as more and more information is captured. Eventually, your computer's memory will become full, and Crosstalk will begin to overwrite the older information. You can avoid this by saving the data on disk, as discussed later in the chapter.

To terminate capture to memory, type

CAPTURE −

Crosstalk will then display

Capture off

on the status line.

You can also suspend the capture function by typing

CAPTURE /

This will resume the capture function if it's currently paused, and pause the function if it's currently on. By default, Crosstalk sets the F5 key to give the CAPTURE / command. Unless you have changed the function key assignments given in the STD.XTK file, pressing F5 can be a quick way of pausing and resuming the capture function.

If you turn the capture function on, record some data in the capture buffer, and then turn the capture function off again, the information will remain in the buffer. However, the next time that you turn the capture function on, the existing data will be erased. You can also erase the information in the buffer by using the ERASE command, as discussed at the end of this section.

## Retrocapture

Another form of the CAPTURE command allows you to "retrocapture" data. Suppose that you have been on line for a while, and you suddenly realize, as some important information scrolls off the screen, that you did not have the capture function on. This is where retrocapture comes in. Crosstalk maintains a circular buffer containing the last 4,096 characters received or transmitted. This buffer is kept up to date whether the capture function is on or off. You can copy the data stored in this circular buffer into the capture buffer, thereby retrieving at least some of the information that you thought you had lost. To do this, enter

CAPTURE <

This command not only captures information that has already been received or transmitted, but also leaves the capture function on, so that new information will continue to be captured until you turn the function off.

Crosstalk will announce the successful copy of the circular buffer with the message

Retro-capture complete

You can also retrocapture a specific number of lines by following the command with a number. For example, to retrocapture 20 lines, enter

CAPTURE <20

Note that once you have turned the capture function on, you cannot use retrocapture. You can invoke retrocapture only when the capture function is off.

## Erasing the Capture Buffer

If you no longer need the information in your capture buffer, you can erase it by entering

ERASE

Crosstalk will give you the prompt

Really erase buffer? Press Y or N:

If you want to change your mind, press N; otherwise, press Y.

# Reviewing the Captured Data

You can display the information in the capture buffer while you are still on line or, probably less expensively, after you have logged off.

## Displaying the Buffer's Status

To see how much space is left in the capture buffer, and other information about the status of the buffer, enter

CSTATUS

Crosstalk will display the current number of text lines and characters in the buffer, the amount of space remaining, and the amount of space on the current disk. Figure 8.1 shows a sample of the data displayed by the CSTATUS command used from the terminal screen while capturing data from CompuServe.

*Using the
CSTATUS
command
from the
terminal
screen to
show the
status of the
capture
buffer.*

```
                              Capture status

         Captured: 15 lines, 0K characters, buffer approximately 0% full

         Space on logged disk:    444K free on drive C:

   -




 Esc for ATtention, Home to SWitch    Capture On, 271K free    On: 00:01:09
```

## Displaying the Buffer's Contents

If you want to examine the contents of the whole capture buffer, enter

TYPE

You can have Crosstalk include line numbers at the beginning of each line by entering

TYPE #

If you want to review only part of the buffer, you can specify the lines to be displayed with the TYPE command. For example, to look at lines starting with line 100, enter

TYPE #100

If you use the TYPE command from the terminal screen, the lines will be displayed continuously, and they may scroll faster than you can read them. To suspend the display, press Ctrl-S; begin it again by pressing Ctrl-Q.

If you use the TYPE command from the status screen, only nine lines will be displayed at a time, and Crosstalk will prompt you to press Enter to see more lines. Pressing Esc instead will terminate the display. Figure 8.2 shows a sample of a capture buffer's contents displayed by entering the TYPE command from the status screen.

## Searching the Capture Buffer

If you are looking for a particular piece on information in the capture buffer, you can have Crosstalk scan through the buffer for you. To have Crosstalk search through the buffer, use the CSTATUS command followed by the word or phrase that you want to locate. For example, suppose that you were looking through an index that you captured to memory for references to IBM. You can enter

CSTATUS IBM

and Crosstalk will display the first reference to IBM in the buffer, together with the surrounding text. It will also prompt you to indicate whether you want to continue to search for more references to IBM.

As an example, Figure 8.3 shows the result of using the CSTATUS command to search for the string *xtalk* in a list of subjects of messages on CompuServe.

Even though turning the capture function off does not erase the capture buffer, and you can still view its contents

**Figure 8.2:**

*Using the TYPE command from the status screen to display the contents of the capture buffer.*

```
┌──── CROSSTALK - XVI Status Screen ────┐        On line

NAme    CSERV                              LOaded   none loaded
NUmber  591-6041                          CApture  On

┌──── Communications parameters ────┐   ┌──── Filter settings ────┐
SPeed  300    PArity None  DUplex  Full    DEbug    Off   LFauto   Off
DAta   8      STop   1     EMulate None     TAbex    Off   BLankex  Off
POrt   1                   MOde    Call     INfilter On    OUtfiltr On

┌──── Key settings ────┐                ┌──── SEnd control settings ────┐
ATten  Esc          COmmand ETX (^C)     CWait    None
SWitch Home         BReak   End          LWait    None

┌──────── Contents of file C:TEMP. ────────┐

17682:  XMODEM HELP           S 2 / Comm. Software

17683:  max80                 S 0 / General

17684:  bobsterm pro          S 2 / Comm. Software

17686:  OVERSEAS CALLS        S 0 / General
        3 replies _
███ More to come...  press ENTER: _
```

by using the TYPE command, you cannot search the capture buffer using the CSTATUS command when the capture function is off.

## Saving to Disk

If you use the CAPTURE command to capture data, that information will be lost when you leave Crosstalk or turn off your computer. You can retain the captured data by saving it to disk, either directly or from the capture buffer. As with saving to memory, all information passing through, whether typed by you or received from the remote computer, will be saved.

## Capturing to Disk

To capture data and save it in a disk file rather than in memory, use the CAPTURE command followed by a file name. For example, if you want to save the data to a file on drive B called MYFILE, you would enter

CAPTURE B:MYFILE

**Figure 8.3:**

*Searching for the string* xtalk *in the capture buffer using the CSTATUS command.*

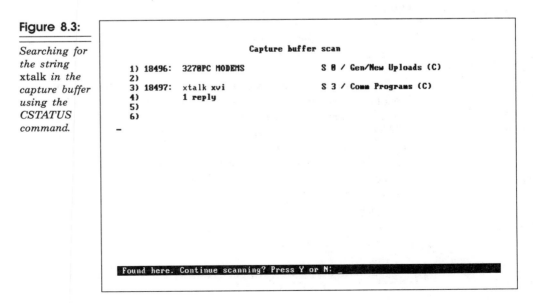

```
                          Capture buffer scan
    1) 18496:  3270PC MODEMS              S 0 / Gen/New Uploads (C)
    2)
    3) 18497:  xtalk xvi                  S 3 / Comm Programs (C)
    4)         1 reply
    5)
    6)
    _




    Found here. Continue scanning? Press Y or N: _
```

If the file MYFILE already exists, Crosstalk will warn you and ask whether you want to overwrite it or add to the end of it by means of the prompt

> B:MYFILE. already exists. Press A to add to it, or E to erase it first.

If at this stage you change your mind, you can press Esc instead, and Crosstalk will give you the message

> Cancelled

If you know that MYFILE exists and that you want to overwrite it, you can tell Crosstalk not to prompt you with this warning by entering

> CAPTURE B:MYFILE/E

You can also tell Crosstalk to append the data to the end of the existing in MYFILE, by entering

> CAPTURE B:MYFILE/A

If the disk becomes full while you are capturing data, Crosstalk will warn you and then start capturing to memory. This will probably give you time to send the appropriate command to the remote computer to stop sending while you find another disk.

When you have saved enough data and you want to close the file, turn the capture function off by entering

> CAPTURE –

Capturing to disk has the advantage of allowing you to record a larger amount of data, and it also protects you from losing all the information in the event of a power loss. However, since the information is not in memory, you cannot review and search through it in the same way that you can when it's in the capture buffer. If you want to use these features, you should capture the information to memory, review it in the buffer, and then save it to disk, as described below.

## Saving the Capture Buffer

You can save the capture buffer to disk by using the WRITE command with a file name. If the file is not on the default drive, precede the file name by the drive name. For example, to copy the capture buffer to MYFILE on drive B, enter

WRITE B:MYFILE

Crosstalk gives you the opportunity to save the capture buffer to disk whenever you enter a command that would delete it, including the command to exit the program. Crosstalk gives the message

Information is still in the capture buffer. Do you want to save it? (Y/N)?

If you type Y, Crosstalk will ask you for a file name. If you don't want to save the information, type N.

## Capturing and Saving Screens

Another data-capturing facility that Crosstalk provides is the capability to capture to memory or save a screen image.

### Capturing a Screen to Memory

In addition to the capture buffer, Crosstalk has a *snapshot buffer*. This buffer is used to hold a copy of a screen image for later review. The command for creating a snapshot of the entire 24 lines of the screen is

SNAPSHOT 24

You can retain an image of only part of the screen by following the SNAPSHOT command with a smaller number of lines.

To see the saved screen, simply enter

SNAPSHOT

There is no way to save the snapshot buffer to disk or to add it to the main capture buffer. Also, the SNAPSHOT command only operates on the terminal screen. If you use it from the status screen, it will still copy the terminal screen to the snapshot buffer.

## Saving a Screen to Disk

You can use the PICTURE command to copy the current screen to a disk file. This is handy when you're receiving or transmitting one screen at a time. Follow the command with a file name. For example, to save the screen to MYFILE on drive B, enter

    PICTURE B:MYFILE

You can also use the /E and /A commands to erase or append to an existing file, just as you use the CAPTURE command to save data to disk.

Like the SNAPSHOT command, the PICTURE command can be used from either the terminal or status screen, but it will save the terminal screen in either case. You cannot use the PICTURE command while the capture function is on.

# 9

# Transmitting Text Files

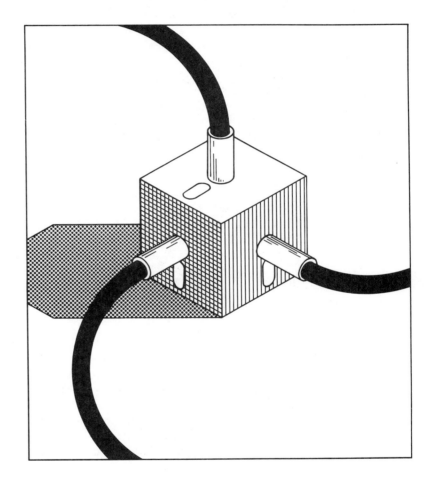

As well as being able to receive data and capture it in a file, Crosstalk can also transmit data from a file to another computer. This chapter describes the SEND command and other commands that affect the transmission of text. Note that the methods discussed in this chapter are not appropriate for the transmission of nontext data, such as spreadsheets or programs; for these types of files, you will need to use a communications protocol, as discussed in the next chapter.

## The SEND Command

You can use the SEND command to transmit text files from your PC to another computer. For example, to transmit MYFILE on drive B, enter

    SEND B:MYFILE

However, some computer systems cannot accept an unaltered IBM PC file sent as one continuous stream of characters. The rest of this chapter explains how to use Crosstalk's delay and filter parameters to modify the transmission to suit most other types of computer systems.

## Delay Parameters

Some computer systems are limited in how quickly they can receive data. Others can receive only one line at a time, and they will send a message when they are ready for the next one. This is generally because they expect to be receiving data from a person typing at a keyboard rather than from a computer sending continuous bursts of transmission from a disk file. Crosstalk has various commands that you can use to handle these problems, as described below.

### Waiting Between Each Line

If you are communicating with a system that sends a prompt when it is ready to accept the next line of text, use the LWAIT command to tell Crosstalk to wait for that prompt. The form of the command that you should use depends on the type of prompt the remote system transmits. You can have Crosstalk wait for a fixed-length prompt, a variable-length prompt, or an incoming character. LWAIT can also be used to tell your computer to ignore incoming prompts and send lines at fixed intervals.

**Waiting for a Fixed-Length Prompt**  Some remote systems send the same prompt after each line. This prompt could be one character, such as a question mark, or several words, such as

Enter Next Line

By using the LWAIT PROMPT command, you can tell Crosstalk to wait until a fixed number of characters (including spaces) has been received before sending the next line. For example, to tell Crosstalk to wait for the three-word prompt above before transmitting the next line, enter

LWAIT PROMPT 15

You may have to add one character to the length of the prompt if the remote system sends a carriage return with it (e.g., the example above would be 16 characters instead of 15).

An easier way of achieving the same effect is by using the command

LWAIT LEARN

This command tells Crosstalk to count the number of characters in the prompt received from the remote system and then to wait for that amount before sending each line.

When you enter the LWAIT LEARN command, Crosstalk will send the first line of the file and ask you to press the spacebar when you are ready to send the second line. Meanwhile, it will count the characters transmitted by the other computer. Once you have pressed the spacebar and Crosstalk has computed the length of the prompt, it will continue sending the file, waiting for the same number of characters to be received between each line.

**Waiting for a Variable-Length Prompt**  Some remote systems do not send the same prompt after each line is received. For example, you may receive the prompt

Enter first line

and then

> Continue. Leave two blank lines to finish

One way to deal with such prompts is to tell Crosstalk to wait for a prompt from you before sending each line. To do this, enter

LWAIT MANUAL

Crosstalk will ask you to press the spacebar when you are ready to send each line. Figure 9.1 illustrates this prompt.

Another way of handling variable-length prompts is to have Crosstalk wait for a given amount of time after the last character is received. The LWAIT QUIET command will tell Crosstalk to wait until no character has been received from the remote system for a specified delay of seconds before sending the next line. The delay is measured in tenths of a second. For example, to tell Crosstalk to wait for 2 seconds of quiet between each line, enter

LWAIT QUIET 20

If the prompts sent by the remote system are of different lengths, but they consistently end with the same character, you can also use the method described below.

**Figure 9.1:**

*The prompt displayed by the LWAIT MANUAL command.*

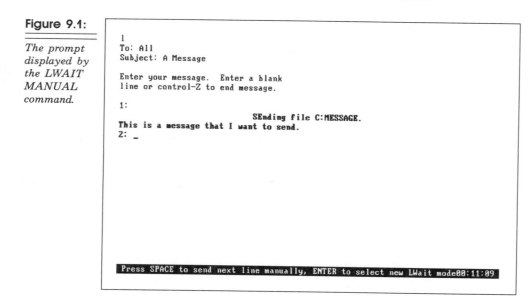

```
1
To: All
Subject: A Message

Enter your message.  Enter a blank
line or control-Z to end message.

1:
                           SEnding file C:MESSAGE.
This is a message that I want to send.
2: _




                                                 
 Press SPACE to send next line manually, ENTER to select new LWait mode00:11:09
```

**Waiting for an Incoming Character**   In some cases, the remote system will end its prompts with the same character. You can tell Crosstalk to wait until that specific character is received before sending each line by using the LWAIT C (CHARACTER) command. For example, one of the Compu-Serve text editors prompts you for each line by sending the line number, followed by a colon. To have Crosstalk wait for the colon, enter

LWAIT C:

If the remote system sends a carriage return after its prompts or by itself to signal that it is ready for each line, use the special command

LWAIT ECHO

This tells Crosstalk to wait for a carriage return.

**Ignoring Incoming Prompts**   It is also possible to tell Crosstalk to wait for a fixed delay between each line and to ignore any prompts received. Again, the delay is measured in tenths of a second. For example, to wait for 1½ seconds between each line, enter

LWAIT DELAY 15

The default condition for the LWAIT parameter is LWAIT DELAY 0; i.e., sending lines one after another without any delay.

## Waiting Between Each Character

If the receiving system processes incoming characters very slowly, you may want to tell Crosstalk to wait for a fixed delay between each character. To do this, use the CWAIT command.

Like LWAIT DELAY, CWAIT tells Crosstalk to wait for a fixed amount of time between transmissions. However, unlike LWAIT, CWAIT measures time in thousandths of a second rather than in tenths. For example, to tell Crosstalk to wait for five thousandths of a second between each character, enter

CWAIT 5

The second form of CWAIT tells Crosstalk to wait for the last character transmitted to be echoed back before sending the next one. The command is

CWAIT ECHO

This command can only be used in full-duplex communications, where each character is echoed back by the remote computer. Note that CWAIT ECHO will really slow down communications if the two computers are a long distance apart, since each character has to travel to the remote system, be processed, and travel back again before the next character is sent.

## Filter Parameters

Some computer systems can only accept data in certain forms. Crosstalk provides commands that you can use to filter the outgoing text so that it is in the appropriate form for the other system.

### Converting to Uppercase

Some systems, such as those interfacing with the TELEX network, will accept only uppercase characters. Others may accept characters in any form, and then impose a surcharge on your bill for converting lowercase characters to uppercase.

To have Crosstalk translate all characters that it transmits from a text file into uppercase, enter

UCONLY ON

before using the SEND command. This command does not affect any punctuation marks in the file.

When the file transmission is completed, turn the function off by entering

UCONLY OFF

### Blank Lines

If you are sending data to a system that translates a blank line as the signal for the end of the transmission, you will need to have Crosstalk filter out any blank lines in the text file. The command for this is

BLANKEX ON

This function converts the blank lines into a line consisting of one character space.
To turn the function off, enter

BLANKEX OFF

## Tab Characters

If the receiving system does not accept tab characters in text files, you can have Crosstalk convert them by entering

TABEX ON

This function will replace the tab character with an equivalent number of spaces.
To turn the function off, enter

TABEX OFF

## Line Feeds

As discussed in Chapter 4, some computer systems will both move to the beginning of the line and move down a line when a carriage return is received. If you are communicating with such a system and do not want Crosstalk to send a line feed following a carriage return, enter

OUTFILTER ON

To resume transmission of the line-feed character, enter

OUTFILTER OFF

The commands discussed in this chapter are used for sending text files to other computers. The procedures for protocol file transfers are described in the next chapter.

# 10

## File-Transfer Protocols

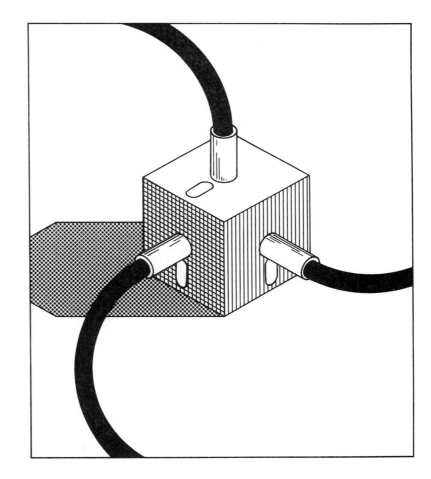

As you've learned in previous chapters, standard text files can be transferred using the SEND and CAPTURE commands. However, if you are transferring other types of files, you may have to use a *file-transfer protocol.*

A file-transfer protocol is a standard for transferring data between two computers other than as a straight stream of ASCII text characters. The main features of file-transfer protocols are error checking and encoding of binary data. Crosstalk has its own file-transfer protocol and supports the XMODEM and Kermit protocols as well. You'll learn how to use these file-transfer methods in this chapter.

## Error Checking and Binary-Data Encoding

In order to check for errors, protocols divide the data to be transferred into blocks, usually of the same length. Each block also incorporates information such as the block number and an error-correcting code. Usually, when the receiving computer detects an error during a block transfer, it sends a message to the sending system, which will retransmit the block automatically.

Another feature of most file-transfer protocols is that they can convert binary data into ASCII form. Since some computers and communications channels can only accept ASCII data, you may have to use this feature to convert binary-data files, such as spreadsheets and computer programs, in order to transmit them.

## Transferring Files Between Crosstalk Systems

Crosstalk offers its own protocol for transferring files between two computers running Crosstalk. This type of file transfer will work with Crosstalk XVI, which runs on the IBM PC and compatible computers, as well as the other versions of the program that run on CP/M-based computers. This means that you can use Crosstalk's protocol for transfers between your PC and a CP/M system.

## Sending and Receiving Files

When you use Crosstalk's protocol, one system must be in answer mode and the other in call mode. All commands must be entered from the computer that is in call mode.

During a file transfer using Crosstalk's protocol (or any other type of protocol), you will not see the file displayed on the screen. Instead, you will see a summary of what is happening. The summary includes the block number, percent complete, consecutive errors found in the block, and the total errors. Figure 10.1 shows a sample of a screen displayed while a protocol file transfer is in progress.

**Setting the Mode**   Before you begin transferring data, use the PMODE command to tell Crosstalk which type of remote system it is talking to. If it is communicating with a remote CP/M system, set

        PMODE 1

If the other computer is a PC-DOS or MS-DOS system, set

        PMODE 2

**Figure 10.1:**

*A sample Crosstalk screen displayed while transferring files using a protocol.*

```
                        Receiving C:PROGNAME.EXE

        ┌──────────┬────────────┬───────────────┬──────────────┐
        │ Block #  │ % complete │ Consec. errors │ Total errors │
        ├──────────┼────────────┼───────────────┼──────────────┤
        │    12    │     8%     │     none      │     none     │
        └──────────┴────────────┴───────────────┴──────────────┘




             PROTOCOL TRANSFER UNDERWAY -- Press Esc to cancel
```

**Transmitting Files**  When you are ready to transmit a file to another Crosstalk system, use the XMIT command, followed by the drive designator and the name of the file that you want to send. The file name can include wild-card symbols (e.g., an asterisk to represent all remaining characters and a question mark to represent a single character) for transmitting multiple files. You can also tell the remote system to save the received files on a particular disk drive by following the file name with a drive letter. For example, the command

XMIT B:*.BAS C:

transmits all files with the extension .BAS on the current directory on drive B and causes the remote system to save them on its drive C.

**Receiving Files**  If you want to have your computer receive a certain file or files from a remote Crosstalk system, use the RQUEST command, followed by a file name. The requested file name can also include wild-card symbols for receiving multiple files and can be followed by a drive name to tell Crosstalk where to save the received files. For example, the command

RQUEST B:*.BAS C:

requests all the .BAS files on the other computer's current directory on drive B and saves them on drive C of your computer.

## Error Checking and Block Size

Like other file-transfer protocols, Crosstalk's divides files up into blocks for error-checking purposes. If the receiving system finds errors in a block, the file-transfer summary will look something like Figure 10.2.

When errors are found, the block is retransmitted automatically. Crosstalk's error report does not mean that there is anything wrong with your file. However, if you see that there are many errors, you may have a bad connection and should try again. The consecutive errors portion of the file transfer summary means that errors were found in consecutive blocks. For

**Figure 10.2:**

*The screen display when errors are found.*

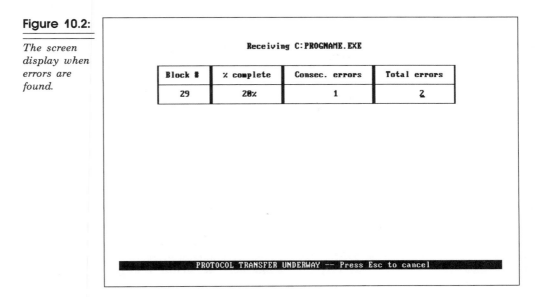

In the figure: Receiving C:PROGNAME.EXE

| Block # | % complete | Consec. errors | Total errors |
|---------|-----------|----------------|--------------|
| 29 | 28% | 1 | 2 |

PROTOCOL TRANSFER UNDERWAY -- Press Esc to cancel

example, 3 consecutive errors mean that the last three blocks each contained at least one error.

The default size of a block is 256 bytes (set as size 1). You can increase the size of the blocks in multiples of 256 bytes up to a maximum of 2,560 bytes (set as size 10). For example, to increase the block size to 512 bytes, enter

    BKSIZE 2

In some cases, increasing the block size can speed up file transfers. However, when there is an error in a larger block, it takes longer to retransmit it. Also, there is a greater likelihood of errors occurring in larger blocks. This won't be a problem if the line is very "clean" (for example, when the two computers are directly connected together), so if you know that errors are very unlikely, it is a good idea to increase the block size.

## An Example of a Remote File Transfer

Imagine that your colleague, Bill, on the other side of the country, has a program file that you need. Both of you have PCs running Crosstalk and 1,200 bps Hayes-compatible modems. The following is a sample scenario for transferring the file.

1. Bill copies the file that you want to receive into the current directory and enters the following commands:

   ```
   SPEED 1200
   DATA 8
   PARITY N
   PWORD CHEESE
   NAME Welcome to Bill's Machine
   PMODE 2
   MODE ANSWER
   COMMAND ^C
   GO
   ```

   These commands set a baud rate of 1,200, 8 data bits, and no parity. The password is CHEESE, and the computer will display the greeting message *Welcome to Bill's Machine* when the connection is made. The PMODE is 2 because the other computer is a PC. The MODE ANSWER command puts this computer in answer mode, which means that it will answer the telephone. The COMMAND ^C means that you will press Ctrl-C when you want to give instructions to Bill's computer, and GO tells the computer to begin waiting for the call.

2. Bill calls and tells you the password, his computer's number, and the file name.

3. You set up your computer to receive the file by entering the following commands:

   ```
   SPEED 1200
   DATA 8
   PARITY N
   NUMBER (415) 123-1234
   ANSWERBACK ON
   FKEYS 4 CHEESE ¦
   PMODE 2
   GO
   ```

   These commands set the appropriate baud rate, data bits, and parity, and enter the telephone number (415) 123-1234. ANSWERBACK ON, followed by FKEYS 4 CHEESE ¦, causes your computer to respond automatically to the other computer's prompt for a password by sending CHEESE, which is stored in function key

F4. The PMODE is 2 because the other machine is a PC, and the GO command tells Crosstalk to dial the number.

4. Once the connection has been established, you press Esc to put your version of Crosstalk in command mode, and then enter

    RQUEST PROGNAME.EXE

    to instruct your version of Crosstalk to request the other computer to transmit the file PROG-NAME.EXE.

5. When the transfer is complete, you terminate the session by entering

    BYE

## An Example of a Local File Transfer

Now imagine that you are running Crosstalk on a CP/M computer with 8-inch disk drives and a serial port, and you want to transfer some BASIC files from that machine to your PC. The BASIC files are on drive B of the CP/M-based computer. You would use the following procedure:

1. Connect the two machines together by means of an RS-232 cable. You will probably need a *null modem* connector (available from many computer stores for a few dollars) that enables two computers to communicate. For full information about connecting the computers, see *The RS-232 Connection* by Joe Campbell (SYBEX 1984) or my *Mastering Serial Communications* (SYBEX 1986).

2. Load Crosstalk on your PC.

3. Enter the following commands.

    SPEED 1200
    DATA 8
    PARITY N
    PMODE 1
    GO LOCAL
    RQ B:*.BAS
    QUIT

These commands set a baud rate of 1,200, 8 data bits, and no parity. The PMODE is 1 because your computer is communicating with a CP/M system, and the GO LOCAL tells Crosstalk that there is no modem. The PC requests all the files on drive B with the extension .BAS and will save them with the same names.

## Using the XMODEM Protocol

XMODEM is a file-transfer protocol devised by Ward Christensen, and it was designed for transferring data between microcomputers. It was not intended for micro-mainframe or long-distance file transfers, but because it is so widely available, it has been used for those purposes. For example, XMODEM can be used to send or receive data from CompuServe.

XMODEM incorporates division of data into blocks and error checking, but it does not handle conversion of binary data into ASCII. If you want to transfer binary data through a communications channel that only accepts ASCII data, you cannot use XMODEM.

With earlier versions of Crosstalk, long-distance communications with XMODEM did not work because, although XMODEM's standard time delay for reporting errors was fine for local file transfers, it was insufficient for longer distances. This problem has been corrected in later versions of Crosstalk.

To transmit a file using the XMODEM protocol, use the XXMODEM command, followed by the file name. For example, to send MYFILE on drive B, enter

    XXMODEM B:MYFILE

To receive a file, enter RXMODEM, followed by a file name. You cannot use wild-card symbols to transfer multiple files at one time.

## Using the Kermit Protocol

Kermit is a file-transfer protocol devised at Columbia University in New York. It was designed for transfers between microcomputers and larger computers, and it is much more powerful than XMODEM. Kermit can handle conversion of binary data into ASCII data for communications purposes, and it can be used to transmit several files at once. The Source is one system that supports the Kermit protocol.

## Transmitting Files

To transmit one or more files to a remote system, use the XKERMIT command, followed by a file name. The file name can include wild-card symbols. For example, the command

    XKERMIT *.COM

transmits all files in the current directory with the extension .COM.

## Receiving Files

With some versions of Kermit, commands as well as data can be sent to a remote computer. These commands are known as *server commands*. Not all computers that support Kermit will accept server commands, so there are different Crosstalk commands for receiving files from systems that do accept server commands and those that do not.

To receive one or more files from a system supporting Kermit server commands, use the GKERMIT command. Follow it with a file name, which can include wild-card symbols.

To receive a file from a remote system that does not support server commands, use the RKERMIT command. Only one file at a time can be received. You do not need to add a file name after the command because the file name will be sent by the remote system. The normal procedure is to instruct the remote computer to start the transfer, then put Crosstalk into command mode and enter

    RKERMIT

RKERMIT is the command that you should use to receive data from The Source.

## Other Kermit Commands

The other Crosstalk commands for the Kermit protocol are summarized below:

| Command | Function |
|---|---|
| KERMIT PSIZE: $X$ | Enables you to set the Kermit packet size to $X$ bytes. You should not use this command unless you are very familiar with the way in which Kermit operates. |
| KERMIT CQUOTE: % | Enables you to change the Kermit control quoting character to the character % (or whatever character you type in its place). The control quoting character is the character used to precede encoded control characters. |
| KERMIT BQUOTE: % | Enables you to change the binary quoting character to the character % (or whatever character you type in its place). The binary quoting character is the character used to precede bytes in which the eighth bit is 1. |
| KERMIT EOL % | Enables you to change the end-of-line character to % (or whatever character you type in its place). |
| KERMIT TIMEOUT X | Sets the Kermit time-out period to $X$ seconds. |
| KERMIT LIST | Lists the current Kermit settings. |
| KERMIT GET *fname* | Works the same as GKERMIT followed by a file name. |

| | |
|---|---|
| KERMIT SEND *fname* | Works the same as XKER- MIT followed by a file name. |
| KERMIT RECV *fname* | Works the same as RKER- MIT followed by a file name. |
| KERMIT FINISH | Ends the current Kermit session. |

For more information about Kermit, refer to my book *Mastering Serial Communications* (SYBEX 1986).

# 11

# Terminal Emulation

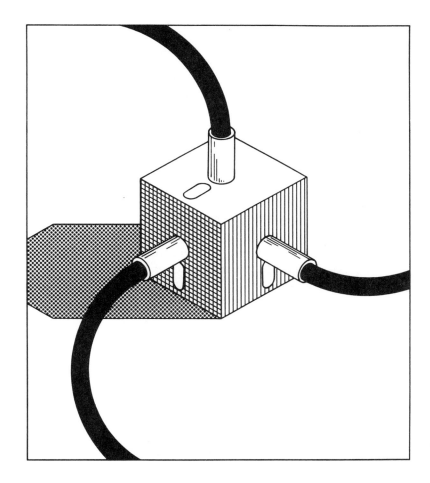

A terminal is a device that facilitates the communications between humans and computer systems. Its function is to allow the user to send information to the computer and the computer to display or print information for the user.

There are many types of terminals of various degrees of sophistication. They can be as simple as a printer and keyboard combination or complex enough to process data themselves.

Since a microcomputer has the basic components of a computer terminal (a keyboard and a screen), it can be used as a terminal. One of the advantages of this is that it gives you the ability to save data to disk for later processing. In order to use your PC as a terminal, you need a program that provides terminal-emulation capabilities, such as Crosstalk. In this chapter, we'll review the various types of terminals, and then discuss how to use Crosstalk for terminal emulation.

# Types of Terminals

The simplest type of terminal consists of only a printer and keyboard, without a screen. Each line is printed as it comes in. The most common of this type of terminal is the Teletype. However, most modern terminals use a cathode-ray tube (CRT) to display the text on a screen like the one on your PC.

## CRTs in Teletype Mode

The simplest form of CRT acts rather like a printer. Each line is displayed on the screen as it comes in, and the display scrolls up one line at a time, like a Teletype. Terminals acting in this way are said to be in Teletype mode, and sometimes are called *glass TTYs*. In fact, a printer terminal and a CRT in Teletype mode both respond to the computer in the same way, except that a CRT receives and processes characters faster.

Almost all PC-DOS and MS-DOS functions (such as COPY and DIR) work in Teletype mode. Each line is displayed below the last until the text gets to the bottom of the screen, and then the new lines are added to the bottom as the other lines scroll up.

## Full-Screen Processing

The next stage up from a glass TTY is a terminal with full-screen processing capability. This means that it can display characters at any location on the screen, rather than just on the next available line. Also, the terminal can display characters with various attributes, such as inverse-video, underlined, or blinking. The combination of these features enables the terminal to produce much more sophisticated displays. Most commercial PC programs (including Crosstalk itself) use full-screen processing for their displays.

To provide full-screen processing, the computer sends special sequences of characters to the terminal to tell it how to handle the display. One sequence may mean "clear the screen," and another may mean "turn on inverse video." These are known as *escape sequences* because they commonly start with the Escape character (ASCII 27).

Unfortunately, not all terminals use the same escape sequences. The computer must know which type of terminal you have in order to send the correct sequences. And some computer systems can use only one type.

## Smart Terminals

The terminals described above are all known as *dumb terminals* because they cannot process any of the data. *Smart terminals* are those that can do more than just display characters and transmit user keystrokes. For example, some have the ability to process forms; they require the user to enter the information into the fields of the form, then send the data to the computer when the user presses the Enter key.

Crosstalk cannot emulate a smart terminal. However, it can emulate several different types of dumb terminals, as described in the rest of this chapter.

# Crosstalk and Terminal Emulation

Crosstalk has the ability to emulate a number of popular terminals. In fact, the program is always emulating a terminal because, in its default mode, it emulates a Teletype—acting as a glass TTY.

When you use Crosstalk's terminal-emulation facility, your PC will appear to the remote computer (called the *host*) as the selected type of terminal. This means that Crosstalk will respond to incoming escape sequences in the same way that the emulated terminal would. In addition, when you press certain keys to send special characters, Crosstalk will transmit to the host the same codes that the real terminal would send.

To have Crosstalk emulate a terminal, use the EMU-LATE command, followed by an abbreviation for the terminal. Crosstalk displays the current setting of the EMULATE command in the communication parameters section of the status screen. Figure 11.1 shows a sample status screen displayed when Crosstalk is emulating an IBM 3101 terminal. The default setting is EMULATE None.

## Emulating Televideo Terminals

Crosstalk can emulate most of the features of the Televideo 910/920 series of terminals. However, the function keys

**Figure 11.1:**

*A sample screen displayed when Crosstalk is emulating an IBM 3101 terminal*

```
┌──── CROSSTALK - XVI Status Screen ────┐        Off line

 NAme                              LOaded   C:STD.XTK
 NUmber                            CApture  Off

┌──── Communications parameters ────┐   ┌──── Filter settings ────┐
 SPeed 1200   PArity None  DUplex  Full    DEbug   Off   LFauto   Off
 DAta  8      STop   1     EMulate IBM 3101 TAbex   Off   BLankex  Off
 POrt  1                   MOde    Call     INfilter On   OUtfiltr On

┌──── Key settings ────┐          ┌──── SEnd control settings ────┐
 ATten  Esc            COmmand ETX (^C)     CWait   None
 SWitch Home           BReak   End          LWait   None

┌──────── Available command files ────────┐

 1) STD
 _


 Command? _
```

are not emulated, nor is block mode. Crosstalk's manufacturer suggests that you program Crosstalk's function keys to have the same functions as those of the Televideo terminal if you need to use them.

The command to enter Televideo-emulation mode is

    EMULATE TV1 920

## Emulating an IBM 3101 Terminal

Crosstalk can emulate an IBM 3101 ASCII terminal, including its function keys PF1 through PF8 (your PC's F1 through F8). The cursor-movement keys on your numeric keypad also will work the same way as those on the 3101. Similarly, if you press Num Lock, the keys will send the codes for the numbers rather than those for cursor movement. Since the Home key sends the Home sequence of the 3101, Crosstalk automatically reassigns the Switch key function to Shift-Home.

The command to emulate an IBM 3101 is

    EMULATE IBM

## Emulating a DEC VT-100 or VT-52 Terminal

You can have Crosstalk emulate a DEC VT-52 or VT-100 terminal; however it cannot simulate all the features of the VT-100. These features are not included: 132-column mode, smooth scrolling, split screen, and double-high and double-wide characters. Whether this is important will depend on your applications software; not all software makes use of these features.

When the Num Lock function is off, you can use the cursor-movement keys on the numeric keypad to simulate those of the VT-100. If Num Lock is on, then the keys will have their numeric values. As with IBM 3101 terminal emulation, the Home key sends the VT-100's sequence, so Crosstalk automatically reassigns the Switch key to Shift-Home.

To emulate a VT-100 terminal, use the command

    EMULATE VT

To emulate a VT-52 terminal, enter

    EMULATE 52

## Emulating Other Terminals

To emulate an Adds Viewpoint terminal, enter

EMULATE ADDS

To emulate a Texas Instrument (TI) 940 terminal, use the command

EMULATE 940

# A Sample Terminal-Emulation Session

This section describes a sample terminal-emulation session. Imagine that you are using your PC as a terminal to a minicomputer or mainframe. The host uses DEC VT-100 terminals, and the program that you need to run does not require any of the terminal's special features that Crosstalk cannot emulate. Your PC is directly connected to the minicomputer (i.e., you are not using modems). The session would involve the following steps:

1. Press the Home key to bring up the status screen.

2. To set the baud rate to 9,600, enter

   SP 9600

   You can run as fast as you like because the machines are directly connected.

3. To emulate a VT-100 terminal, enter

   EM VT

4. Commence connection by entering

   GO LOCAL

5. Press Enter (or Return). (A carriage return is commonly sent to the host to start a session.)

6. Enter your password when the host prompts you for it.

7. Do your work.

8. Enter the command to tell the host to terminate the session. This varies from host to host, but it could be

   LOGOFF

9. Press Esc to put Crosstalk into command mode.

10. Tell Crosstalk to terminate on-line mode by entering

    BYE

In the chapters in this part of the book, you have learned how to use Crosstalk's basic commands for sending and receiving data and how to have your PC emulate a terminal. The next part describes how to use command and script files to automate many communications tasks.

# Part 4

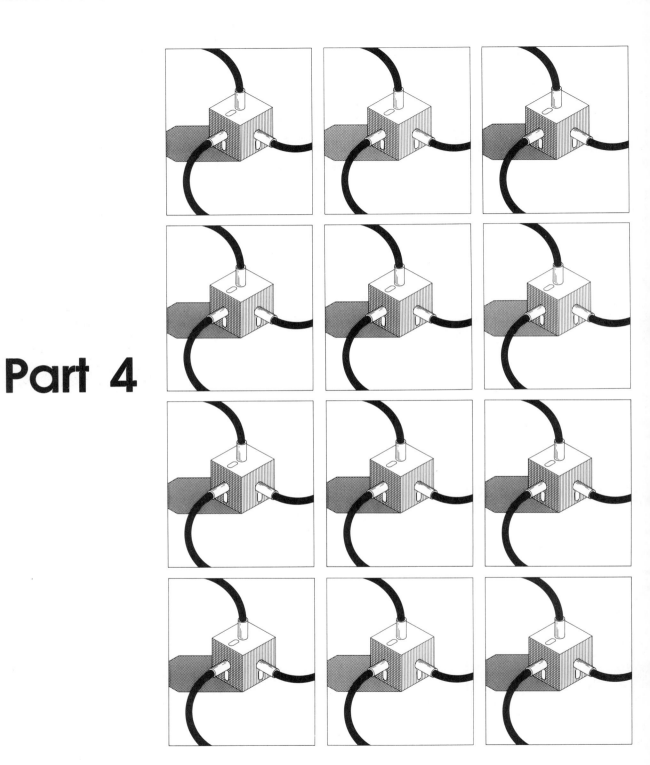

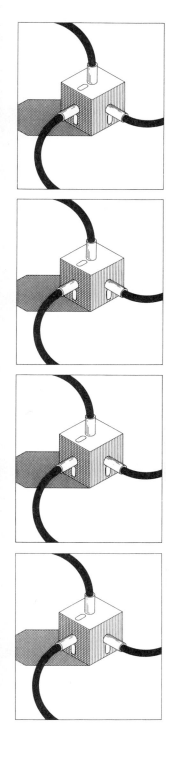

# Automating
# Crosstalk

# 12

# Command Files

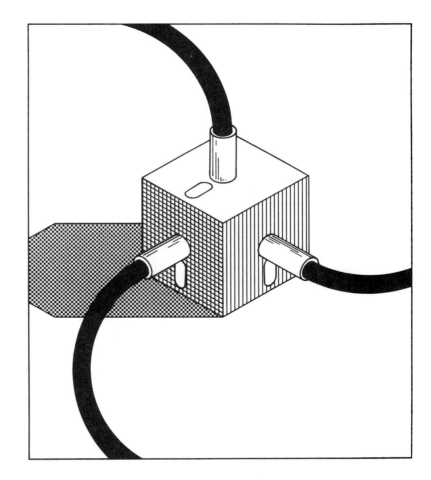

As mentioned earlier, you can give Crosstalk commands directly from the keyboard or from a file stored on disk. Disk files containing Crosstalk commands are known as command and script files. Command files deal with parameters for Crosstalk, such as baud rate, parity, and filter settings, as well as function key assignments. Script files, which we will cover in the next chapter, involve interactions with another computer after the connection has been made.

## Command File Uses

The principal purpose of command files is to save time. Most people who use communications programs access a few other computer systems on a regular basis. Rather than entering the same commands each time, you can merely enter the name of the command file to make the connection. Crosstalk will even display a numbered list of all the command files in your current directory, so that you can select a particular command file by simply entering its number.

The following listing is a typical command file. The comments in the second column are for explanation only; they would not appear in an actual command file.

| | |
|---|---|
| SPEED 1200 | Set the baud rate to 1,200. |
| DATA 8 | Set 8 data bits. |
| PARITY N | Set no parity. |
| NUMBER 123-1234 | Store this as the current telephone number. |
| FK 2 PETER_SECRET | Store *PETER_SECRET* as a password in function key F2. |
| FK 3 71222,1234 | Store user ID 71222,1234 in function key F3. |
| GO | Dial the number and try to make a connection. |

# Creating Command Files

Command files are standard ASCII text files with the extension .XTK. There are two main ways of creating a command file:

- Entering the parameters through Crosstalk and using the SAVE command

- Using a word-processing or text-editing program, either to create a new file or to edit one you created using the SAVE command

## Using the SAVE Command

You can enter all the communications parameters from the keyboard while you are in Crosstalk's command mode, just as we did in the sample session included at the end of Chapter 5. Then, while you're still in command mode, you can instruct Crosstalk to save the current settings in a file by using the SAVE command, followed by a file name. For example, if you want to create a command file named MYFILE to dial the same number that you used in the sample session in Chapter 5, repeat steps 1 through 3, and then enter

SAVE MYFILE

You do not have to give Crosstalk the .XTK extension when you are saving or loading command files. Crosstalk will add the extension for you.

If you· use the SAVE command after you have entered a telephone number with the NUMBER parameter, Crosstalk will automatically conclude the .XTK file with the GO command. If you have not given a telephone number, Crosstalk will assume that your computer is directly connected to the other computer, and it will terminate the file with a GO LOCAL command.

## Using a Word-Processing Program

To create a command file using a word-processing program, you must first instruct the program to produce an

ASCII file. With WordStar, for example, you could create a command file called MYFILE.XTK as follows:

1. Enter WS to invoke WordStar.

2. Press N to select nondocument mode.

3. Enter MYFILE.XTK as the name of the file.

4. Type the following command file:

```
SP 1200
DATA 8
PARITY N
NUMBER 123-1234
GO
```

5. Press Ctrl-K Ctrl-D to save the file.

6. Press X to exit from WordStar.

## Choice of Method

Both methods of creating a command file work equally well. I generally use the SAVE command, since establishing the correct parameters can often be a matter of trial and error. Entering the commands from the keyboard while I'm using Crosstalk allows me to change and resave parameters until they are correct.

The methods can even be combined. You can use your word processor to edit a file created with the SAVE command, or you can use Crosstalk to load a file created with your word processor, change the parameters, and save it with the SAVE command.

# Loading Command Files

There are four ways of loading and running a command file:

- When you load the program itself, enter the name of the command file after Crosstalk's own name. For example, to run our sample MYFILE.XTK command file, enter (from the DOS prompt)

  ```
  XTALK MYFILE
  ```

• Have a file in the current directory called STD.XTK. Crosstalk will run this file automatically each time you load the program.

• Select a command file from the menu displayed on the status screen. When you load Crosstalk by just entering XTALK without a file name, it searches the current directory for all files with the extension .XTK and lists them on a menu (see Figure 2.1). You can choose a file by entering the number next to it.

• Use the LOAD command. For example, you could load and run our sample file by entering

    LOAD MYFILE

Alternatively, you can just type LOAD, and Crosstalk will display a menu of the command files available on your current directory. Note that Crosstalk's LOAD command is equivalent to BASIC's RUN command followed by a file name, rather than to BASIC's LOAD command (which just brings the file into memory). It both loads the file into memory and begins execution of it.

In Part 5 of this book, you'll see some practical examples of command files. Also, you may want to take a look at the command files supplied with Crosstalk for accessing various services.

# 13

# Script Files

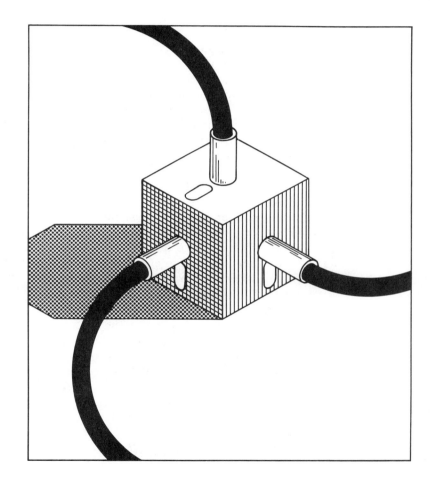

Script files are similar to the command files described in the last chapter. They are created as simple ASCII files that contain lists of commands, one on each line, and are loaded and executed by Crosstalk. However, script files perform a somewhat different function from command files. This chapter describes their uses and explains how to create and run them.

## Script File Uses

Script files help to automate the process of interacting with a remote computer after communication has been established. They enable you to define the messages to be sent to the remote system and the actions to be taken when messages are received from that computer. Script files can also contain commands that tell Crosstalk to prompt you for certain information.

Because script files simplify the communications process, using them can save you money by reducing the time that you spend on line. With some on-line services charging in excess of $60 per hour, your savings can add up to a significant amount quite quickly.

Another advantage of script files is that they can be combined with command files to simplify communications tasks for users who are not very familiar with Crosstalk. The files will run the program so that a new user can concentrate on the purpose of the call.

Figure 13.1 shows a short script file that illustrates how you can automate a communications task. The individual commands are explained later in this chapter. The sample script file starts at the point at which communications have been established with a remote system.

## Creating Script Files

Script files are created using a word-processing or text-editor program. They must be saved as ASCII files, with the extension .XTS.

Before creating your own script files, you may want to take a look at the NEWUSER.XTS file that comes with

**Figure 13.1:**

*A typical
script file.*

```
WAIT Quiet 20              Wait for 2 seconds of silence on the line.
REPLY ^C                   Send Ctrl-C to the host computer.
WAIT String "ID"           Wait for the host to ask for your ID number.
REPLY "123,1234"|          Send the ID number 123,1234.
WAIT String "PASSWORD"     Wait for host to ask for the password.
REPLY "SECRET"|            Send the password.
WAIT String "Command?"     Wait for the host to ask for a command.
CA REPORT.SAV              Capture to file called REPORT.SAV.
REPLY "REPORT2"|           Ask the host for report number 2.
WAIT String "Command?"     Wait for the end of the report.
CA-                        Turn off capture.
REPLY "LOGOFF"|            Give the logoff command to the host.
WAIT String "End"          Wait for the host to end the session.
BYE                        Hang up the phone.
```

Crosstalk. This file creates script files for accessing a number of popular information utilities. To run it, enter

DO NEWUSER

The best way to create a script file is first to perform the procedure that you want to automate, with the capture function on. You can then print out a transcript of the communications session and refer to it as you create your script file.

The commands in a script file do not have to be on separate lines. If you want to include several commands on a line, separate them by a space, a colon, and another space. For example, WAIT and REPLY commands might appear like this:

WAIT STRING "ID" : REPLY "71334,1234"

You can also include comments in a script file. Any line starting with a semicolon is ignored when the script file is executed. It's a good idea to include plenty of comments to remind yourself or another user what each section of the file does.

## Loading and Running Script Files

You can load and run a script file by using one of the following methods:

- Give it the same name as the command file that establishes communication, and the script file will run once the command file is completed. For example, if you have a command file called CSERV.XTK that dials CompuServe and a script file called CSERV.XTS that logs onto that service, the script file will run automatically once connection with CompuServe's computer is established. Examples of using command and script files in this way are provided in Part 5. If you have a number of script files that you use with each service, then you will probably want to give the one for logging on the same name as the command file.

- Use the DO command, followed by the file name. This command works like the LOAD command for command files, as described in the last chapter. For example, to load and run a file named MYSCRIPT.XTS, enter

    DO MYSCRIPT

- Select the script file from the menu displayed by the DO command alone. If there is no current script file in memory, enter

    DO

and Crosstalk will show you a list of available script files. Figure 13.2 shows a sample of a menu displayed by the DO command.

## Suspending and Terminating Script Files

If you want to terminate a script file that is currently being processed, enter

DO –

To resume processing of a script file that is currently in memory, enter

DO

Remember, if you use DO alone when there *isn't* a script file currently in memory, Crosstalk will display a menu of available script files.

To terminate processing of a script file from within the file itself, end it with the command

ABORT

**Figure 13.2:**

*A sample menu displayed by the DO command.*

```
┌─────── CROSSTALK - XVI Status Screen ───────┐        On line

MAme   COMPUSERVE                         LOaded   C:CSERV.XTK
NUmber 591-6041                           CApture  Off
┌────── Communications parameters ──────┐  ┌────── Filter settings ──────┐
SPeed 1200   PArity None   DUplex Full      DEbug    Off    LFauto   Off
DAta  8      STop   1      EMulate None      TAbex    Off    BLankex  Off
POrt  1                    MOde    Call      INfilter On     OUtfiltr On

┌────────── Key settings ──────────┐       ┌────── SEnd control settings ──────┐
ATten  Esc            COmmand ETX (^C)       CWait    None
SWitch Home           BReak   End            LWait    None

┌────────────────── Available script files ──────────────────┐
1) CONF      2) CSERV      3) READMAIL    4) SENDMAIL    5) STOCK
_

Enter number for file to use ( 1 - 5 ): _
```

The file will stop at this point, and control will be returned to the user.

## Communicating with Script Files

Script files can automate the process of sending and receiving messages. The command for sending messages is REPLY, and the command for receiving the remote computer's responses is WAIT.

### Sending Messages

You can use the REPLY command to send a string of text to the remote computer. This might be a password or a command to run a particular program. For example, the CompuServe command for entering the programmers' special interest group is GO PROGSIG. To send this command followed by a carriage return (¦), your script file might include the line

REPLY GO PROGSIG ¦

You can also use the REPLY command to send a text string that is assigned to a particular function key (see Chapter 7). For example, to send the text string assigned to F7, your script file would contain the line

REPLY @F7

## Waiting for Responses

The WAIT command tells Crosstalk to wait until a particular condition has been met, and then continue with the next line in the script file. To automate the dialog between computers, you would define the condition as the remote system's response.

There are several versions of the WAIT command, as described below.

| Command | Function |
|---|---|
| WAIT Echo | Requires Crosstalk to wait until a carriage return is received from the remote system. |
| WAIT Quiet $X$ | Requires Crosstalk to wait until no characters have been received for $X$ tenths of a second. Use this when you are not sure of the remote system's response. For example, many systems give you some sort of news bulletin when you log on. Using an appropriate WAIT Quiet command would tell Crosstalk to wait until the bulletin has finished. |
| WAIT Delay $X$ | Requires Crosstalk to wait for a certain amount of time ($X$ tenths of a second) before proceeding to the next line. |
| WAIT Char '$X$' and WAIT For '$X$' | Require Crosstalk to wait until a particular character is received. For example, to tell Crosstalk to |

wait for a colon, enter

> WAIT Char ':'

or

> WAIT For ':'

This could also be abbreviated to WAIT C: or WAIT F:. Note that there is no space between the C or F and the character that you want to wait for.

WAIT Prompt *X*

Requires Crosstalk to wait until *X* number of characters have been received from the remote computer. Use it when you know that the computer always responds with a particular string and you know how many characters there are in the string.

WAIT String *Text*

Requires Crosstalk to wait until a particular text string has been received from the remote computer. Use this when the response is always the same. For example, to log onto a computer that asks you for a password, the script file might include

> WAIT String "Enter Password"
> REPLY SECRET_WORD ¦

The WAIT String command ignores case.

WAIT Until
HH:MM

Tells Crosstalk to wait until a fixed time of day. The military (24-hour clock) format is used. For example, to tell it to wait until ten past two in the afternoon, enter:

> WAIT Until 14:10

WAIT Manual — Returns control to the user. At this point, you can type text in directly from the keyboard to interact with the remote computer or enter Crosstalk commands. To resume execution of the script file, make sure that you're in command mode, then enter the DO command.

It is possible to construct a complete communications session by using a script file consisting only of REPLY and WAIT commands (Figure 13.1 shows a file like this). You would include the NUMBER and GO commands in a command file to dial the system, and then begin the script file.

# Interacting with the User

In addition to being able to program Crosstalk to communicate with a remote computer, you can have it interact with you or any other user. You can give messages (or menus), obtain input, switch screens, clear the screen, and sound an alarm. The commands for these functions are described below.

## Presenting Messages

You can present a message or menu to the user by using the MESSAGE command. This command displays one or more lines of text on the user's screen. MESSAGE is on a line by itself, followed by the line (or lines) to be displayed and ending with a line that contains only a single period. For example, to send the message *Dialing CompuServe* to the user, the script file would include

```
MESSAGE
Dialing CompuServe
.
```

To display a menu to the user, the script file might say

```
MESSAGE
Press R to Retry
```

Press A to Abandon

## Obtaining User Input

You can obtain either a single keystroke or a line of text from the user by means of the ASK command. This command allows you to construct script files that can be reused for different purposes, which greatly increases their flexibility.

To ask the user to press a key, follow the command with the request for a keystroke. For example, the script file might contain the line

ASK Press R to retry, A to abandon.

Figure 13.3 shows how the MESSAGE and ASK commands can be used to display a menu from which the user can select options. The SCREEN and CLEAR commands used in that example are explained in the next section. You can program the appropriate response to the user's selection by "jumping" to the corresponding commands, as described later in this chapter.

If you want the user to enter a string of text rather than one character, you have to assign the user's response to a function key or function-key combination. For example, to ask for a password and assign the response to function key F3, the script file would contain the line

ASK @F3 Please enter your password.

Then you could send that information to the remote computer by using the line

REPLY @F3

**Figure 13.3:**

*Displaying a menu with options.*

```
SCREEN T
CLEAR
MESSAGE

    Welcome to the Program
    ----------------------

    P) Proceed with the Program
    H) Help
    Q) Quit
  .

ASK Press a key to make your choice.
```

Incidentally, this example illustrates a good security feature. If you store a password as part of a script file (the sample script files supplied with Crosstalk do this), it will be easily accessible to others. Many people believe that the only place where passwords should be stored is in one's head. Accordingly, it is a good idea for a script file to use the ASK command to obtain the password rather than saving it on disk.

## Preparing the Screen

When you include messages in your script file, you will want to prepare the screen for their display. You can switch between the status and terminal screens by using the SCREEN command. To switch to the status screen, you would write

    SCREEN S

To change to the terminal screen, you would write

    SCREEN T

To clear the current screen, use the CLEAR command. If the current screen is the terminal screen, the whole screen is cleared. If it is the status screen, the lower half of the screen is cleared, and the status information remains.

## Sounding an Alarm

In some script files, you may want to include an alarm to let the user know when his or her attention is required. To sound an audible alarm, use the ALARM command.

There are four different alarm tones that can be used, from 1 through 4. For example, to create tone 1, the script file would read

    ALARM 1

# Program Flow Commands

In its command and script files, Crosstalk actually embodies a simple programming language. The files contain lists of instructions that Crosstalk follows, can have variables (in the form of function-key strings), and provide for interaction with a user.

So far, all our examples have been of commands that Crosstalk follows in sequence as it steps through the script file. But if the program is to behave differently depending on the user's response, as when a menu of options is presented, there must be some way of jumping to different parts of the script file. This is called *program flow control*, and Crosstalk provides several facilities for it.

## Labeling Lines

Instead of using line numbers for referencing program parts, Crosstalk allows you to give names, or labels, to lines. Then you can instruct Crosstalk to jump to that line (using the JUMP command, as described in the next section) by referencing the label.

Use the LABEL command, followed by the name, to label a line. Lines that have labels do not perform any functions other than containing the label. The line with the label should immediately precede the script file section that you want Crosstalk to jump to. For example, at various points in a script file, you may give the user the option of logging off. To be able to jump to the section of the script file that contains the log-off commands, you would use the LABEL command in a line immediately preceding the log-off section. If you wanted to name that section LOGOFF, the line would read

    LABEL LOGOFF

Using meaningful words for labels will help you remember what the labeled sections do. The only rule for labels is that they must all begin with a letter.

## Jumping to Lines

In a script file, the simplest way of passing control to a different section is by using the JUMP command followed by the label of the line where Crosstalk should continue. For example, to jump to the log-off section mentioned above, you would include the line

    JUMP LOGOFF

If, in the course of processing a script file, Crosstalk comes to a reference to a label that does not exist, it will display on the status line

Label not found in script file . . script suspended. press
   ENTER: _

When you press Enter, you will receive the regular prompt

Command?

You can tell Crosstalk to resume processing the script file at the next statement by entering

DO

As mentioned earlier, you can use the ASK command to obtain input from the user. To have the program jump to different sections depending on the user's input, you can use the *conditional* JUMP command. In this form, the at sign (@) represents the user's response. For example, suppose that you used the ASK command to get an input of A, B, or C. You could write sections of the script file for each of the choices and give the sections labels of CODE-A, CODE-B, and CODE-C, respectively. You could then use the command

JUMP CODE-@

This would cause the program to jump to the section labeled CODE-A if the user pressed the A key, CODE-B if the user pressed the B key, or CODE-C if the user pressed the C key.

If the user accidentally pressed a different key, the program would just continue to the next statement in the file. You can catch the error by having that next line ask the user to try again (with the MESSAGE command), and return the program to the beginning of the menu section (with the JUMP command followed by a label). That part of the script file would look like this:

MESSAGE
Invalid key: try again

JUMP MENU

## Including Conditions

You can also use the IF command to tell Crosstalk to do different things depending on different events. For example, another way to include a conditional JUMP command is to precede it with the IF command. To use this technique in the example described above, you would include the lines

```
LABEL MENU
ASK Press A B or C
IF A JUMP CODE-A
IF B JUMP CODE-B
IF C JUMP CODE-C
MESSAGE
Invalid key: try again
  .
JUMP MENU
```

The IF command can even be used with multiple conditions. For example, you can cause a jump if the user presses one of several keys by including the line

```
IF ABC JUMP CODE-A
```

This will cause a jump to the portion of the script file labeled CODE-A if the user presses either the A, B, or C key. No spaces or commas are allowed in the key sequence (ABC in the example above).

You can also use the minus sign (−) with the IF command to create a negative condition. For example, if you wrote

```
IF −ABC CLEAR
```

then Crosstalk would clear the screen if the user pressed any key *other* than A, B, or C.

You can have the program respond differently depending on whether or not you are on line by using the dollar sign with the IF command. For example, the line

```
IF $ CLEAR
```

would clear the screen if your computer is on line to another computer. The $ simply represents the state of being on line.

Figure 13.4 shows a program that uses the IF command for a conditional jump, a negative condition, and a condition based on being on line. If you select the Quit option from the menu presented by the script file, it tests whether you're still on line, and if so, jumps to the log-off section of the script file (elsewhere in the file). If you are not on line, the next sequential statement will be executed, and will give Crosstalk the command to terminate.

## Skipping Lines

Rather than using the LABEL and JUMP commands to move to another section of a script file, you can use the SKIP command to skip over a given number of lines. Follow the command with the number of lines that you want to skip. For example, the line

    SKIP 6

would have the program continue with the seventh line following it. You cannot skip backwards, or beyond the end of the file.

You could include a conditional skip by preceding the SKIP command with an IF condition. Figure 13.5 shows a script file that includes a conditional skip as well as two different forms of conditional jumps.

The script file in that figure first asks you to press a key. If you press Q for Quit, it asks you to confirm your choice, and if you do not press Y, it goes back to the request to press a key. If you do not press Q, it jumps to the section of the script file that is labeled CODE- followed by the letter that you pressed.

**Figure 13.4:**

*Detecting on-line state.*

```
LABEL MENU
MESSAGE
        C .... Continue
        Q .... Quit
  .
ASK Enter Selection
IF Q JUMP EXIT
IF -C JUMP MENU
JUMP CONTINUE
LABEL EXIT
IF $ JUMP LOGOFF
QUIT
```

## Restarting the File

You may want to restart a script file from the beginning. The RWIND command does just this, rather like rewinding a cassette and starting it again. You might use this command, for example, to obtain a series of similar reports from an on-line service.

## Repeating Actions

The WHEN commmand can be used to have the script file repeat an action each time that you receive a message from the remote system. Follow the command with the message that you are waiting for, surrounded by quotation marks. For example, you might often receive the message

Press M for More

You can instruct Crosstalk to transmit an M every time that you get this message by including the line

WHEN "Press M for More" REPLY M

The WHEN command stays in effect until it is cancelled, which is done by the command

WHEN −

If you want the WHEN command to execute only the first time that the text string is received, you must cancel it immediately after it executes. The cancelling command should be included at the end of the script file line containing the WHEN command. For example, the line

WHEN "Password" REPLY FRED : WHEN −

would send the password FRED only the first time that a password is requested.

**Figure 13.5:**

*Including a conditional SKIP command.*

```
LABEL MENU
ASK Press a key to indicate your choice
IF -Q SKIP 2
ASK Quit selected: Press Y to confirm
IF -Y JUMP MENU
JUMP CODE-@
```

WHEN always ignores case, so that the above example would recognize not just *Password*, but also *PASSWORD* or *password*. It also ignores any blanks in the incoming text string.

Finally, note that only one WHEN command can be active at any one time.

## Sending a Break

The SBREAK command causes a break signal to be transmitted to the remote computer. Break signals are described in Chapter 3.

## Programming with Script Files

As you have seen, Crosstalk's script file facilities can be used to create quite complex and powerful programs. Some examples of the use of script files are presented in the last part of this book. In particular, you may like to look at the example of accessing the Official Airline Guide (OAG) under CompuServe in Chapter 15. The script file in that example repeatedly executes a section of code until a particular string is received, and then it breaks out of the loop and continues with other commands.

# 14

# Crosstalk for Programmers

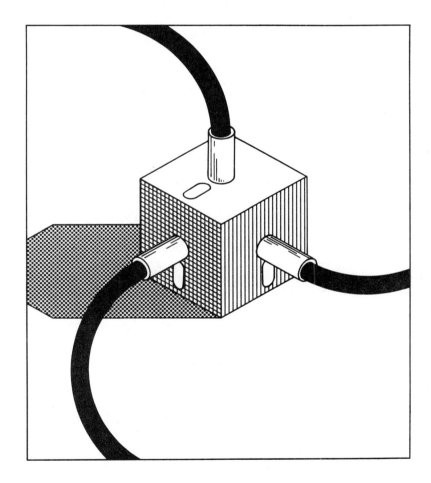

In the two previous chapters, you learned about Crosstalk's command and script files. By creating these files, it's possible to automate a complete Crosstalk session, including logging onto a remote system, transmitting data, and logging off. If you invoke Crosstalk with the name of a command file (for example, XTALK MYFILE), then the program can run without your intervention.

Chapters 12 and 13 explain how to create command and script files using Crosstalk commands. If you're a programmer, another way to create these files is by writing a program in a high-level language such as BASIC. Crosstalk has one other feature of particular interest to programmers: the DEBUG command. Both of these aspects of the program are discussed in this chapter.

## Generating Command and Script Files

You can write a program for a specific application that creates Crosstalk command and script files as part of the routine. For example, suppose that you wanted to automate a procedure for searching a database system. You could write a BASIC program that asked the user for all the necessary information and then created the command and script files that would have Crosstalk dial a remote computer, search through the database, save the information in a text file, and log off. Finally, the BASIC program could read the text file and format it. The whole process could be controlled by a batch file, such as

```
BASICA GETINFO
XTALK BASFILE
BASICA PRINTREP
```

where GETINFO.BAS and PRINTREP.BAS are BASIC program files on your disk, and BASFILE.XTK and BASFILE.XTS are command and script files created by the BASIC program.

Figure 14.1 illustrates a sample BASIC program to generate Crosstalk files. This program accesses a fictitious database, and it is in outline form only.

By using a high-level programming language to obtain information from a user, you can incorporate some

**Figure 14.1:**

*A sample BASIC program to generate command and script files.*

```
10 REM BASIC PROGRAM TO CREATE CROSSTALK FILES
15 QT$=CHR$(34):' The quotation character
20 GOSUB 100:    ' ASK FOR NAME TO CHECK
30 GOSUB 200:    ' CREATE THE XTK FILE
40 GOSUB 300:    ' CREATE THE XTS FILE
50 SYSTEM
100 REM ASK USER FOR NAME
105 REM
110 PRINT "PLEASE ENTER THE NAME TO CHECK "
120 INPUT NM$
130 RETURN
200 REM CREATE THE XTK FILE
205 REM
210 OPEN "TEST.XTK" FOR OUTPUT AS #1
220 PRINT #1, "SPEED 1200"
230 PRINT #1, "DATA 8"
240 PRINT #1, "PARITY N"
250 PRINT #1, "NU 123-1234"
260 PRINT #1, "GO"
270 CLOSE #1
280 RETURN
300 REM MAKE THE XTS FILE
305 REM
310 OPEN "TEST.XTS" FOR OUTPUT AS #1
320 PRINT #1, "WAIT String "; QT$; "PASSWORD"; QT$
330 PRINT #1, "REPLY MY_PASS|"
340 PRINT #1,"WAIT String "; QT$; "Name to check"; QT$
350 PRINT #1, "CAPTURE DOWNLOAD/A"
360 PRINT #1, "REPLY ";
370 PRINT #1, NM$; "|"
380 PRINT #1, "WAIT String "; QT$; "End of Report"; QT$
390 PRINT #1, "CAPTURE OFF"
400 PRINT #1, "REPLY LOGOFF"
410 PRINT #1, "WAIT String "; QT$; "End of Session"; QT$
420 PRINT #1, "BYE"
430 PRINT #1, "ALARM"
440 PRINT #1, "QUIT"
450 CLOSE #1
460 RETURN
```

sophisticated features, such as more attractive screen displays. The information can then be passed to Crosstalk through a script file.

## The DEBUG Command

Programmers can use Crosstalk's DEBUG command to gain more information about the data transmission. You can use this command to display the incoming control characters, as well as to ascertain the status of the RS-232 control signals.

### Using DEBUG to Display Incoming Characters

During some transmissions, you may want to be able to analyze all the characters, not just the displayable ones.

This information can be useful, for example, to someone writing software on a mainframe. You could use Crosstalk's terminal-emulation facilities to have your PC act as a terminal, and then analyze the output coming from the mainframe to the terminal.

Crosstalk offers three different displays of incoming control characters: hexadecimal, ASCII mnemonics, and control-character symbols.

**Displaying Hexadecimal Digits**   You can display all characters as hexadecimal digits by entering

> DEBUG HEX

Figure 14.2 shows an example of a Crosstalk hexadecimal screen display.

**Displaying ASCII Mnemonics**   You can display the transmitted control characters as their ASCII mnemonics (e.g., CR for a carriage return) by entering

> DEBUG ASCII

Figure 14.3 shows an example of a Crosstalk ASCII mnemonic screen display.

**Figure 14.2:**

*A sample Crosstalk hexadecimal screen displayed by the DEBUG HEX command.*

```
[6E][64][73][20][77][69][74][68][20][74][68][65][69][72][0D][0A][72][65][73][70][
[65][63][74][69][76][65][20][64][65][73][63][72][69][70][74][69][6F][6E][73][20][
[74][6F][20][61][73][73][69][73][74][20][79][6F][75][20][69][6E][20][75][73][69][
[6E][67][20][43][6F][6D][70][75][53][65][72][76][65][2E][0D][0A][0A][20][54][20][
[2D][20][54][4F][50][0D][0A][20][47][6F][65][73][20][64][69][72][65][63][74][6C][
[79][20][74][6F][20][74][68][65][20][66][69][72][73][74][20][70][61][67][65][20][
[20][54][4F][50][29][20][6F][66][20][43][6F][6D][70][75][53][65][72][76][65][2E][
[0D][0A][20][4D][20][2D][20][4D][65][6E][75][0D][0A][47][69][66][65][73][73][20][
[62][61][63][6B][20][74][6F][20][74][68][65][20][6D][65][6E][75][20][70][61][67][
[65][20][74][68][61][74][20][70][6F][69][6E][74][73][20][74][6F][20][74][68][65][
[20][63][75][72][72][65][6E][74][20][70][61][67][65][2E][0D][0A][20][41][20][73][
[69][6E][67][6C][65][20][3C][43][52][3E][20][77][69][6C][6C][20][61][6C][6C][73][6F][
[20][72][65][74][75][72][6E][20][74][6F][20][74][68][65][20][6C][61][73][74][20][
[6D][65][6E][75][20][69][66][20][74][68][65][72][65][0D][0A][20][69][73][6E][27][
[74][20][61][6E][20][6E][65][78][74][20][70][61][67][65][2E][0D][0A][20][48][20][
[6F][72][20][3F][20][2D][20][48][45][4C][50][0D][0A][20][44][69][73][70][6C][61][
[79][73][20][74][68][69][73][20][69][6E][66][6F][72][6D][61][74][69][6F][6E][2E][
[20][4F][74][68][65][72][20][48][45][4C][50][20][6D][65][73][73][61][67][65][73][
[73][20][61][72][65][61][20][61][76][61][69][6C][61][62][6C][65][0D][0A][20][77][
[69][74][68][69][6E][20][73][70][65][63][69][66][69][63][20][73][65][72][76][69][
[63][65][73][2E][0D][0A][0A][20][47][20][2D][20][47][6F][0D][0A][20][47][6F][20][
[4F][20][70][61][67][65][20][2D][20][47][4F][20][64][69][72][65][63][74][6C][79][
[20][74][6F][20][61][20][73][65][72][76][69][63][65][2E][0D][0A][20][54][61][6B][
[65][73][20][79][6F][75][20][69][
```

```
Esc for ATtention, Home to SWitch    Capture Off      On: 00:01:32
```

**Displaying Control Symbols**  You can instruct Crosstalk to show control characters preceded by a circumflex ( ^ ), as in ^C for Ctrl-C, by entering

DEBUG CHAR

Figure 14.4 shows an example of a Crosstalk control symbol screen display.

## Using DEBUG to Display RS-232 Signals

DEBUG can also be used to display the handshaking signals currently being sent and received. To use this option, enter

DEBUG RS232

The signals are represented by a display in the lower right-hand corner of the screen, in the format shown in Figure 14.5. In the first two positions (marked T and R in the figure), the last transmitted and received characters are displayed. In the other positions, the numbers are shown in inverse-video if the corresponding circuit is high. The zero represents circuit 20. For example, if your modem is on line to another modem, the carrier detect line (circuit 8) should be high, and the number 8 will be shown in inverse-video.

**Figure 14.3:**

*A sample Crosstalk ASCII mnemonic screen displayed by the DEBUG ASCII command.*

```
LF ]     All Rights Reserved[CR ][LF ][CR ][LF ][CR ][LF ][CR ][LF ][ESC][1;1H[E
SC][2J[ESC][1;1H[ESC][2JCompuServe[ESC][1;77H TOP[CR ][LF ][CR ][LF ][ESC][7;1H 1
 Subscriber Assistance[CR ][LF ] 2 Find a Topic[CR ][LF ] 3 Communications/Bulle
tin Bds.[CR ][LF ] 4 News/Weather/Sports[CR ][LF ] 5 Travel[CR ][LF ] 6 The Elec
tronic MALL/Shopping[CR ][LF ] 7 Money Matters/Markets[CR ][LF ] 8 Entertainment
/Games[CR ][LF ] 9 Home/Health/Family[CR ][LF ]10 Reference/Education[CR ][LF ]1
1 Computers/Technology[CR ][LF ]12 Business/Other Interests[CR ][LF ][ESC][24;1H
[ESC][J![CR ][LF ]CompuServe      CIS-162[CR ][LF ][CR ][LF ]BRIEF COMM
AND SUMMARY[CR ][LF ][LF ]Every command must end with a carriage return.  Pressi
ng the carriage return key[CR ][LF ](which may be marked ENTER on some keyboards
) transmits the command to[CR ][LF ]CompuServe.[CR ][LF ][LF ]In online informat
ion, the carriage return key is represented by the symbol[CR ][LF ]<CR>.  Pressi
ng <CR> at the end of an article returns you to the previous menu.[CR ][LF ][LF
] T - TOP menu page[CR ][LF ] M - previous MENU[CR ][LF ] H or ? - HELP[CR ][LF
] GO word or GO page - GO directly to a service[CR ][LF ] FIND topic - FIND all
references to topic[CR ][LF ] OFF or BYE - sign off[CR ][LF ] S n - SCROLL from
n[CR ][LF ] R - RESEND a page[CR ][LF ] F - FORWARD a page[CR ][LF ] B - BACK a
page[CR ][LF ] N - display NEXT menu item[CR ][LF ] P - display PREVIOUS menu it
em[CR ][LF ] SET option - SET terminal option[CR ][LF ] PER - exit to Personal F
ile Area[CR ][LF ][LF ]Control Character Commands[CR ][LF ][LF ]Note:  These com
mands are entered by pressing two keys together: the Control key[CR ][LF ]and a
letter key.[CR ][LF ][LF ] Control C - Stops the program being used.[CR ][LF ][L
F ] Control O - Discontinues the flow of information to your computer[CR ][LF ]
         or terminal without stopping the curre_
    Esc for ATtention, Home to SWitch          Capture Off           On: 00:00:25
```

**Figure 14.4:**

*A sample Crosstalk control symbol screen displayed by the DEBUG CHAR command.*

```
    RESENDS the current page.  This is useful if the current page has[^M][^J] scrol
   led off the screen or after a HELP command.[^M][^J][^J] FIND topic[^M][^J] Finds
    all index references to a topic and displays a menuized[^M][^J] list with corre
   sponding page numbers.[^M][^J][^J] N - NEXT[^M][^J] Goes to the NEXT item from l
   ast selected menu.  If 5 was the[^M][^J] last choice, N will display item 6.[^M]
   [^J][^J] P - PREVIOUS[^M][^J] Goes to the PREVIOUS item from last selected menu.
    If 5 was[^M][^J] the last choice, P will display item 4.[^M][^J][^J] F - FORWA
   RD[^M][^J] Displays the next page in a series of pages.  A single <CR>[^M][^J] w
   ill do the same thing.[^M][^J][^J] SET option[^M][^J] SETs a terminal display op
   tion.  You can enter SET and be[^M][^J] prompted for the option and setting, or
   enter SET followed[^M][^J] by the option and the setting.[^M][^J][^J]Options and
   settings for the SET command are:[^M][^J][^J] PAG     ON/OFF        paged mode[^
   M][^J] BRI     ON/OFF      brief mode[^M][^J] TTY     *see below   terminal typ
   e[^M][^J] WID     10-255       screen width (columns)[^M][^J] LIN     10-255
      screen length (lines)[^M][^J]  ?      (none)      displays a list of valid o
   ptions[^M][^J][^J]*Settings for TTY are:[^M][^J][^J] VIDTEX     TELERAY     TELI
   DON[^M][^J] DUMCRT     TELETYPE   TRS80[^M][^J] VT100      VT52[^M][^J][^J]SPEC
   IAL may specify terminals that are not in one of the preceding categories.[^M][^
   J][^J] PER or EXIT[^M][^J] EXITs to the Personal File Area.  From some subsystem
   s, EXIT[^M][^J] takes you to the previous menu.[^M][^J][^J] OFF or BYE[^M][^J] D
   isconnects you from CompuServe immediately.[^M][^J][^J] Control Character Comman
   ds[^M][^J][^J] Control characters transmit special commands to the host[^M][^J]
   computer.  These commands are entered by pressing two[^M][^J] keys together:  th
   e Control key and a letter key.[^M][^J][^J]_
   Esc for ATtention, Home to SWitch          Capture Off          On: 00:02:03
```

**Figure 14.5:**

*The format of the display shown by the DEBUG RS232 command*

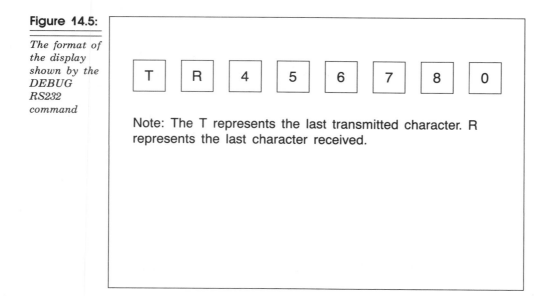

Note: The T represents the last transmitted character. R represents the last character received.

In the last three chapters, you've learned how Crosstalk can be automated through the use of command and script files. The next part of the book shows just how these files can be used to access and communicate with some popular information services.

# Part 5

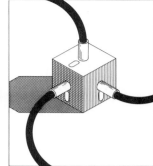
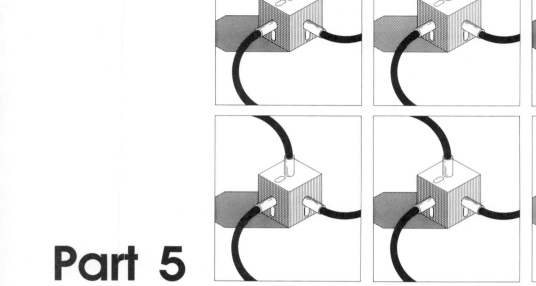
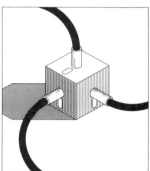
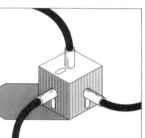
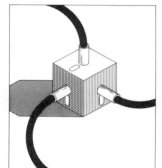
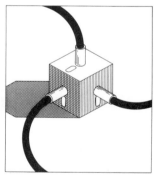
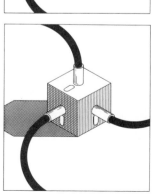
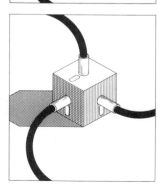
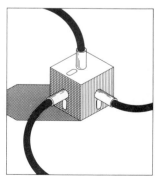

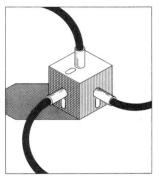

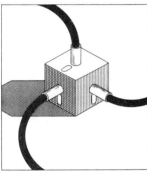

# Using Crosstalk with Information Services

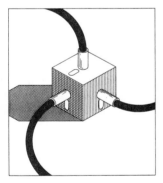

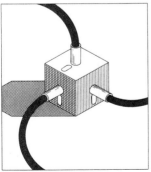

# 15

# Using Crosstalk
# with CompuServe

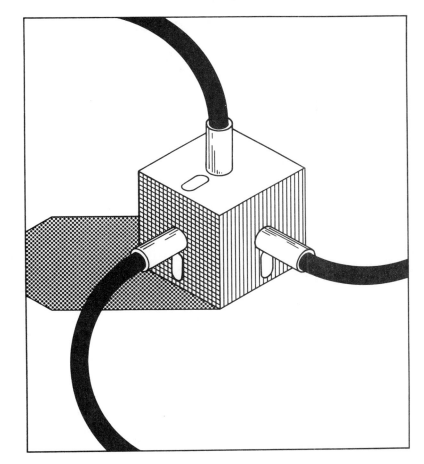

CompuServe is one of the most popular information utilities, and it provides both business and entertainment services. It offers access to many databases, commercial information suppliers (e.g., the Official Airline Guide), special interest groups, games, and an on-line CB simulator channel.

## Accessing CompuServe

CompuServe can be accessed through Tymnet, Telenet, or its own network. You can set baud rates from 300 to 2,400 and either 7 data bits with even parity, or 8 data bits with no parity. I recommend that you use 8 data bits, since that way you can transfer binary-data files using the XMODEM protocol.

The following is a sample command file for accessing CompuServe. You can adapt this file for your own use, as explained in the second column.

| | |
|---|---|
| NUMBER 123-1234 | Insert the local access number for Tymnet, Telenet, or CompuServe's network. |
| DATA 8<br>PARITY NONE | Use these data bit and parity settings if you want to use the XMODEM protocol. |
| SPEED 1200 | Set the appropriate baud rate (from 300 to 2,400). |
| FKEYS C1 MY*NUMBER | Store your ID number in Ctrl-F1. |
| FKEYS C2 MY*PASSWORD | Store your password in Ctrl-F2. |
| EMULATE VT100 | Emulate a VT-100 "dumb" terminal. |
| GO | |

# Logging On

The contents of your log-on script file depend on which network you are using. Examples of files for logging on through CompuServe's network, Telenet, and Tymnet are shown in Figures 15.1, 15.2, and 15.3, respectively.

The files all begin with the command to wait 2 seconds before replying, but the actual replies depend on the system that you are using to access CompuServe. When you

**Figure 15.1:**

*A log-on script file for CompuServe's network.*

```
WAIT Delay 20
REPLY ^C

; User ID
WAIT String "ID"
REPLY @C1
REPLY |

; Password
WAIT String "password"
REPLY @C2
REPLY |

; Tell user we are logged on
SCREEN T
CLEAR
MESSAGE
You are now logged on to CompuSer\
.
```

**Figure 15.2:**

*A log-on script file for accessing CompuServe via Telenet.*

```
WAIT Delay 20
REPLY |
REPLY |
WAIT String "TERMINAL"
REPLY D1|

; Send the code for CompuServe
WAIT F@
REPLY C 202202|

; User ID
WAIT String "ID"
REPLY @C1
REPLY |

; Password
WAIT String "password"
REPLY @C2
REPLY |

; Tell user we are logged on
SCREEN T
CLEAR
MESSAGE
You are now logged on to CompuServe
.
```

**Figure 15.3:**

*A log-on
script file for
accessing
CompuServe
via Tymnet.*

```
WAIT Delay 20

; Terminal type
REPLY "A"

; Service required
WAIT String "log"
REPLY "CIS02"
REPLY |

; User ID
WAIT String "ID"
REPLY @C1
REPLY |

; Password
WAIT String "password"
REPLY @C2
REPLY |

; Tell user we are logged on
SCREEN T
CLEAR
MESSAGE
You are now logged on to CompuServe
.
```

use CompuServe's network, the reply is simply a Ctrl-C
character, and then the user-identification section follows
immediately.

For Telenet, the file sends two carriage returns, waits for
the string *TERMINAL*, and replies D1 carriage return.
Then, to send the code for CompuServe, the file waits for
an at sign (@) and replies C 202202 carriage return.

For Tymnet, the file replies A for the terminal type. To
name the service required, the file waits for the string
*LOG*, and then replies CIS02, followed by a carriage
return.

These script files end with the same user-identification,
password, and message sections. The user-identification sections wait for the user ID to be requested, send the user ID
number stored in Ctrl-F1, and end with a carriage return. The
password sections wait for the string *PASSWORD*, and then
reply with the text stored in Ctrl-F2, followed by a carriage
return. The last section switches to the terminal screen, clears
it, and displays the message

You are now logged onto CompuServe

## Emulating a VT-100 Terminal

The sample command file at the beginning of this chapter
includes an EMULATE VT100 command to tell Crosstalk

to emulate a VT-100 terminal. This helps CompuServe to present more attractive menus and to clear the screen at appropriate places. It is entirely optional, and you could leave out that command if you prefer. If you decide to leave it in, you will have to tell CompuServe that you have a VT-100 terminal. You do this on line by using the following procedure:

1. Enter

   GO TERMINAL

   and CompuServe will display the menu shown in Figure 15.4.

2. Press 2 to select the Setting Your Terminal Type option from the menu. This displays a list of terminals, as shown in Figure 15.5.

3. Press 2 to select the ANSI compatible (VT-100) option.

4. Press Return to display the Terminal Parameters screen, as shown in Figure 15.6.

5. Set the parameters shown in that figure. Note in particular that parity is set to zero. This is to ensure that you can transmit files using the XMODEM protocol.

**Figure 15.4:**

*The Compu-Serve Terminal/ Options menu.*

```
CompuServe       TERMINAL/OPTIONS

  1 Instructions
  2 Setting Your Terminal Type
  3 Setting Your Logon Actions
  4 Setting Delays for Printers
  5 View or Change Current
      Terminal Parameters
  6 Setting your Service options




















  Enter choice ! _
  Esc for ATtention, Home to SWitch        Capture Off        Numeric
```

**Figure 15.5:**

*The Compu-Serve Terminal Type menu.*

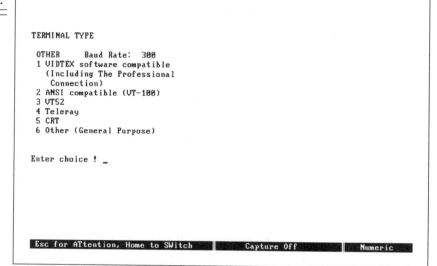

```
TERMINAL TYPE

OTHER     Baud Rate:  300
1 VIDTEX software compatible
  (Including The Professional
  Connection)
2 ANSI compatible (VT-100)
3 VT52
4 Teleray
5 CRT
6 Other (General Purpose)


Enter choice !  _




   Esc for ATtention, Home to SWitch        Capture Off        Numeric
```

**Figure 15.6:**

*The CompuServe Terminal Parameters screen.*

```
TERMINAL TYPE

 VT100     Baud Rate:  300
TERMINAL PARAMETERS
1 Terminal width  80 CHARACTERS
2 Screen size is now   24 LINES
3 Form Feeds are          REAL
4 Horizontal Tabs are     REAL
5 Terminal supports  UPPER/LOWER
6 Caps Lock is            OFF
7 Line Feeds are          SENT
8 Parity is               ZERO
9 Blank Lines are         SENT
10 Inquire for VIDTEX is   OFF




Enter choice !  _
   Esc for ATtention, Home to SWitch        Capture Off        Numeric
```

## Special Interest Groups

CompuServe provides access to special interest groups for a broad range of subjects, from IBM PC Communications (GO IBMCOM) to Human Sexuality (GO HSX). Each group has a bulletin board and a data library, which are both divided into the same sections.

### Using the Bulletin Boards

You can find out the names of the sections in a special interest group's bulletin board (and data library) by using the SN command. As an example, Figure 15.7 shows a list of the sections in the IBM PC Communications forum, as displayed by the SN (Section Names) command.

**Reading the Bulletin Boards**  You can read the messages on a special interest group's bulletin board in a number of ways. You could read all the messages, in forward or reverse order; read just those in a particular section; or search for keywords in the message titles.

The method that I use most often is to search for keywords after reading a list of message titles. You can produce this

**Figure 15.7:**

*A list of the sections in the IBM PC Communications forum displayed by the SN command.*

```
sn

 0 Gen/New Uploads (C)
 1 AuTOsig (C)
 2 Comm Utilities (C)
 3 Comm Programs (C)
 4 Bulletin Boards (C)
 5 Ask the SysOps (C)
 6 Hot Topic (C)
 8 Village Inn (C)

Function:  _




    Esc for ATtention, Home to SWitch        Capture Off        On: 00:01:41
```

list using CompuServe's QSN (Quick Scan, New Messages) command, as follows:

1. Press Esc to enter Crosstalk's command mode.
2. Turn on the capture buffer by entering

   CA +

3. Enter (to CompuServe)

   QSN

4. Wait for the messages to be listed.
5. Turn off the capture buffer by entering

   CA −

The resulting list held in the capture buffer includes all the message titles, along with the number of replies for each message. Since you entered QSN, rather than QS, it only indicates the messages that have been added since you last read the bulletin board. Figure 15.8 shows a sample message listing.

**Figure 15.8:**

*A sample list of bulletin board message titles.*

```
QSN
17871:  Purchasing a modem        S 1 / Comm. Hardware
        1 reply

17872:  amiga online!             S 0 / General

17874:  COMMUNICATIONS            S 0 / General
        1 reply

17875:  BBS                       S 0 / General
        2 replies

17877:  INTERVIEW                 S 0 / General

17879:  mite software             S 2 / Comm. Software

17881:  BITCOM/CALLWAIT           S 2 / Comm. Software
        1 reply

17882:  Co-Sysop                  S 0 / General

Function:  _

Esc for ATtention, Home to SWitch    Capture Off    Numeric
```

You can then use Crosstalk's TYPE command to review the contents of the capture buffer, noting keywords for the messages that you would like to read.

From this point, you can search through the bulletin board for those keywords to find the messages, and then capture them to read later. For example, suppose that you wanted to read a message titled *2400 baud modems*. You would turn on Crosstalk's capture buffer, and then type in the following command to CompuServe:

    RS;S;2400;N

This tells CompuServe to read messages, searching for the string *2400* in the titles, starting with the new messages. After the first message has been displayed, enter NS to tell CompuServe not to stop between messages. When CompuServe completes the search, you would turn off the capture buffer and save its contents to a file. You can read the captured messages later at your leisure, after you've logged off.

**Replying to Messages**  If you find that you want to reply to any of the messages, you can compose your reply (off line, of course) and save it in a file. Then, to leave the reply, log back onto CompuServe, access the appropriate special interest group, and use the CompuServe RE command followed by the message number. This command brings up CompuServe's editor program, which expects you to type in a message at the keyboard. Instead, you can use Crosstalk's SEND command to transmit the file that contains your reply.

The software for the special interest groups (known as SIGWARE) gives you a choice of two editors: SED or EDIT. You select your editor by using the OP command, which displays the User Option menu shown in Figure 15.9. I use EDIT because I find I can transmit a file to it very easily. With SED, line numbers are displayed at the beginning of each line, and you cannot leave blank lines in a message.

## Using the Data Libraries

The data libraries of the special interest groups consist of a variety of items, ranging from discussions made up of

**Figure 15.9:**

*The Compu-
Serve User
Options menu
displayed by
the OP
command.*

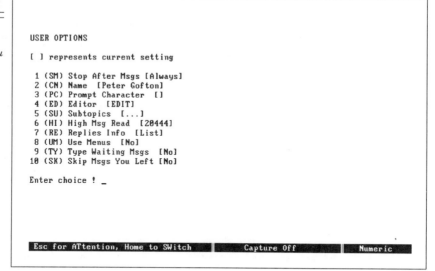

```
USER OPTIONS

[ ] represents current setting

 1 (SM) Stop After Msgs [Always]
 2 (CN) Name [Peter Gofton]
 3 (PC) Prompt Character []
 4 (ED) Editor [EDIT]
 5 (SU) Subtopics [...]
 6 (HI) High Msg Read [20444]
 7 (RE) Replies Info [List]
 8 (UM) Use Menus [No]
 9 (TY) Type Waiting Msgs [No]
10 (SK) Skip Msgs You Left [No]

Enter choice ! _
```

```
Esc for ATtention, Home to SWitch        Capture Off        Numeric
```

messages on the same subject to programs that you can
have CompuServe send to you. There is a data library for
each section in a special interest group.

**Receiving a File**  You would use the following procedure to find
information in a data library and capture it to a file:

1. From the special interest group's bulletin board,
   access the section of the data library that you are
   interested in by entering the DL (Data Library) command followed by the number of the section. For
   example, to enter section 2 of the data library, type

   DL2

2. Use the Browse command to view a list of the files in
   that section by entering

   BRO

3. When you see a file that you would like to read, press
   Esc to enter Crosstalk's command mode.

4. Capture the data file by entering the CAPTURE command, followed by a file name. For example, to save it

to MYFILE, enter

CA MYFILE

5. Tell CompuServe to transmit the file in ASCII format by entering

READ

You don't need to use the XMODEM protocol if you are receiving a standard text file. The procedure for receiving binary-data files is described below.

6. When CompuServe has finished sending the file, press Esc to enter Crosstalk's command mode.

7. Turn off the capture buffer by entering

CA  –

If the file that you want sent is stored in machine-readable form, you will need to use the XMODEM protocol to transfer it. For example, you might be browsing in section 2 of the IBM PC Communications forum's data library (Communications Utilities) and come across the file DSCOPE.ARC. This is a program that enables your computer to act as a communications monitor, as described on the screen shown in Figure 15.10.

You would have to use the following procedure to have CompuServe send the file:

1. Enter to CompuServe

DOWNLOAD

CompuServe displays the Data Library Protocol menu shown in Figure 15.11.

2. Press 1 to select XMODEM, and CompuServe will ask you to start the transfer.

3. Press Esc to put Crosstalk in command mode.

4. Tell Crosstalk to use the XMODEM protocol to receive the file by entering

RXMODEM DSCOPE.ARC

**Figure 15.10:**

*A description of the DSCOPE.ARC program.*

```
[71355,470]
DSCOPE.ARC              27-Jun-86 66795(28512)        Accesses: 53

   Keywords: RS232 LINE-MONITOR EAVESDROPPING DEBUGGING ASYNC

   D'Scope turns a PC into a line monitor, which provides a way of
   "eavesdropping" on a data communications link. Hardware needed is
   two asynch com ports, 256k RAM, mono or color monitor. Useful to
   anyone writing or debugging async com software & to anyone setting
   up & maintaining asynch com circuits. Also useful as a teaching
   aid. [The preceeding was written by D'Scope author Harrison Uhl.

Press <CR> for more !
   Null modem & cable needed.] DL via protocol. Unpack with ARC-E.
   (8-bit)
   -Upl: Nelson Ford-


Disposition ! _
```
```
 Esc for ATtention, Home to SWitch        Capture Off         Numeric
```

**Figure 15.11:**

*CompuServe's Data Library Protocol menu.*

```
DOWNLOAD

Data Library Protocol Menu

Transfer protocols available -

1 XMODEM (MODEM7) protocol
2 CompuServe 'B' protocol
3 CompuServe 'A' protocol
4 DC2/DC4 CAPTURE protocol

0 Abort transfer request


Enter choice !1
Starting XMODEM transfer

Please initiate XMODEM transfer
and press <CR> when the transfer
is complete.
  ▬
```
```
 Command? RXMODEM DSCOPE.ARC_
```

While the file transfer is taking place, Crosstalk displays a summary showing its progress, as illustrated in Figure 15.12. As explained in Chapter 10, this summary shows the number of blocks received and errors detected. When an error is detected, the block is automatically retransmitted. You shouldn't be concerned if there are some errors, but if there are many of them, you probably have a bad connection and should try redialing.

Incidentally, files with an .ARC extension have been specially compressed to save transmission time. They need to be put back into their original form (*unpacked*) by using the ARC-E.COM program. This program can be obtained from the IBM Novice forum (GO IBMNEW), in the Tools section of the data library (DL2), using the XMODEM protocol.

**Sending a File**   You may want to send text and programs of your own to a data library for other people to share. The procedure is the reverse of receiving a file. You select the appropriate data library section (e.g., DL2) and enter the command

UPLOAD

**Figure 15.12:**

*A summary of an XMO-DEM file transfer in progress.*

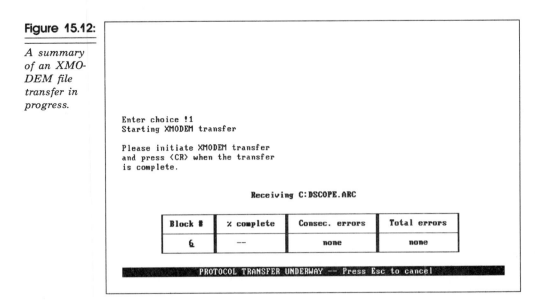

```
Enter choice !1
Starting XMODEM transfer

Please initiate XMODEM transfer
and press <CR> when the transfer
is complete.


                   Receiving C:DSCOPE.ARC
```

| Block # | % complete | Consec. errors | Total errors |
|---------|-----------|----------------|--------------|
| 6 | -- | none | none |

PROTOCOL TRANSFER UNDERWAY -- Press Esc to cancel

You will be asked for the file name and protocol. Again, choose XMODEM, and then use the Crosstalk XXMODEM command to transmit the file.

## Conference and CB Facilities

Some of the special interest groups hold regular conferences on topics of interest to their members. But the most popular conferencing facility is the CB simulator (GO CB).

There is no special procedure for using Crosstalk to access CompuServe's CB. However, if you are using Crosstalk's terminal-emulation feature, you should turn it off during any conference session because it will not allow long lines to wrap around to the next line, and that facility is needed in conference mode. Turn off terminal emulation by entering

EM NONE

To make sure that you don't miss any interesting remarks, you may want to leave the capture buffer on during the whole conference. You can edit the captured file and print it out after you've logged off. Also, with the entire conference session captured to memory, you can search through the capture buffer to find specific items. For example, if you wanted to check on everything someone with the handle CODER said, you could enter to Crosstalk

CS CODER

The program will scan the capture buffer for the string *CODER*, and you can review just those comments.

You also may want to store some commonly repeated expressions in your PC's function keys. For example, the CompuServe command to list users currently on channel 1 is

/UST 1

If you use this command often, you could program it into the Shift-F1 combination by entering to Crosstalk

FKEYS S1 /UST 1

## Using the Official Airline Guide

CompuServe provides access to the Official Airline Guide (OAG), which gives details of flights and fares. It is what CompuServe calls a premium service, meaning that charges are incurred in addition to CompuServe's regular charges. As with all expensive services, it is important to minimize the time spent on line to OAG, and this is where the use of script files can really save you money.

Figure 15.13 shows a sample script file to obtain OAG flight information. The file prompts you for the departure and destination city codes, for the date and time, and for a file in which to save the data. It then selects the OAG database and receives information about all the flights between the cities you selected, on the date you chose, after the time that you selected. The OAG command for the next page of data is a plus sign (+) followed by a carriage return (¦). The script file repeatedly sends this code until the message

NO LATER FLIGHTS

is received from OAG. The script file then exits from OAG and closes the capture file.

This script file is provided as an example only. I have not covered all the eventualities (for example, an invalid city code), and the procedure may have already changed. But it does illustrate the results that can be obtained by using a relatively sophisticated script file.

## Business Information Searches

CompuServe offers many services that provide business and corporate information. Script files are also very useful for obtaining information from these services. As an example, Figure 15.14 shows a script file that gets a quote for a given stock. The script file prompts the user for the code for the stock (e.g., IBM), and then goes to the Quotes section of CompuServe and obtains the current price.

**Figure 15.13:**

*A sample
script file to
receive flight
information
from OAG.*

```
; First ask for the departure city
ASK @S1 Give the code for the departure city

; Now ask for the destination city
ASK @S2 Give the code for the destination city

; Now ask for the date
ASK @S3 Give the date in the format 08 AUG

; Ask for time
ASK @S4 Give the time in the format 600AM

; Ask for the file name
ASK @S5 Give the name of the file to save the data in

; Get confirmation
ASK Press 'Y' to confirm
IF -Y JUMP EXIT

CAPTURE @S5
REPLY GO OAG|
WAIT Delay 20

REPLY 3|
WAIT For '1'
REPLY |

WAIT String "/S"
REPLY /S|

WAIT String "DEPARTURE"
REPLY @S1|

WAIT String "DESTINATION"
REPLY @S2|

WAIT String "DATE"
REPLY @S3|

WAIT String "TIME"
REPLY @S4|

; Set up to break out of the loop when we have seen all the flights that day
WHEN "NO LATER" JUMP OAGEXIT

; Loop getting the next page if information
LABEL LOOP
WAIT String "LINE NUMBER"
REPLY +|
JUMP LOOP

LABEL OAGEXIT
REPLY /Q|

WAIT Delay 20
CAPTURE OFF

LABEL EXIT
CLEAR
MESSAGE
Finished
.
```

**Figure 15.14:**

*A sample
script file to
get a stock
price.*

```
; First ask for company symbol
ASK @S1 Give the company symbol _

; Ask for the file name
ASK @S5 Give the name of the file to save the data in _

; Get confirmation
ASK Press 'Y' to confirm _
IF -Y JUMP EXIT

CAPTURE @S5
REPLY GO QUOTES|

WAIT String "Choice"
REPLY 1|

Wait String "Issue"
REPLY @S1|

WAIT String "Issue"
REPLY |

WAIT Delay 20
CAPTURE OFF

LABEL EXIT
MESSAGE
Finished
.
```

As with the OAG script file, you should be careful with the script file for obtaining stock quotes because the procedure may have changed.

## Logging Off

CompuServe's command to log off is

OFF

What happens after you enter this command depends on how you accessed CompuServe. If you dialed CompuServe directly and responded with a Ctrl-C to the initial connection, CompuServe will disconnect the line when you log off. Crosstalk will then notify you that the carrier has been lost, and ask you to press Enter. You will then be left in Crosstalk's command mode.

If you logged on through a network, CompuServe will return you to the network when you log off. You will have to disconnect the line yourself by using Crosstalk's BYE command.

# 16

# Using Crosstalk
# with The Source

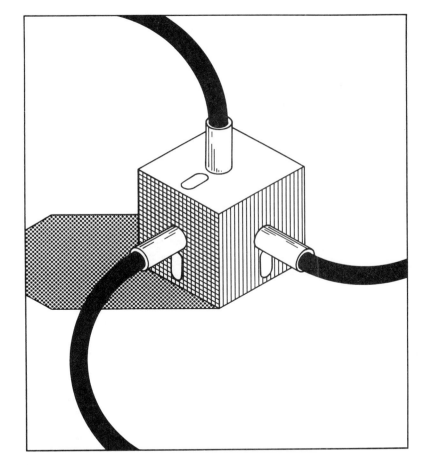

Like CompuServe, The Source is a popular information utility used for both business and entertainment. It offers services in the following six main categories:

- Communications
- News, weather, and sports
- Business and investing
- Education, shopping, and games
- Travel
- Personal computing

Some of The Source's services provide detailed, regularly updated information; some, like games and electronic shopping, are highly interactive; and others, such as electronic mail and computer conferencing, are communication oriented.

## Accessing The Source

To access The Source, set a baud rate from 300 to 2,400 and 8 data bits with no parity. It can be accessed through Telenet, Uninet, or Sourcenet, its own network. Since Uninet is primarily designed for UNIX systems, and Sourcenet is not widely available, the sample files in this chapter are for use with Telenet.

The following is a sample command file for accessing The Source. The second column explains how to adapt the file for your own use.

| | |
|---|---|
| NUMBER 123-1234 | Insert your own local access number. |
| DATA 8 | Set 8 data bits. |
| PARITY NONE | Set no parity. |
| SPEED 1200 | Set a baud rate from 300 to 2,400. |
| FKEYS C1 MY*NUMBER | Save your ID number in Ctrl-F1. |

FKEYS C2 MY*PASSWORD  Save your password in Ctrl-F2.

## Logging On

The contents of your log-on script file will depend on which network you are using. A sample script file for logging onto The Source through Telenet is shown in Figure 16.1. Note that your code for The Source (C 30149 in the sample file) depends on the system that you are assigned to when you subscribe.

## Special Interest Groups

The Source offers access to many types of special interest groups. To access one, type Q to enter The Source's command mode, then type the name of the group. For example, to access the special interest group for IBM personal computers (IBMSIG), enter

Q
IBMSIG

**Figure 16.1:**

*A log-on script file for accessing The Source via Telenet.*

```
WAIT DELAY 20
REPLY |
REPLY |

; Terminal Type
WAIT String "Terminal"
REPLY D1|

; Code for The Source (depends on the system you are assigned to)
WAIT F@
REPLY C 30149|

; User ID
WAIT For '>'
REPLY ID
REPLY @C1
REPLY |

; Password
WAIT String "password"
REPLY @C2
REPLY |

; Tell user we are logged on
SCREEN T
CLEAR
MESSAGE
You are now logged on to The Source
```

## Participating in Conferences

The Source uses the term *conference* very differently from CompuServe. CompuServe's conferences consist of users talking to each other on line, either in one of the special interest groups or through the CB simulator. The Source does not offer such facilities. It uses the term conference to describe collections of messages on a single subject—what CompuServe calls bulletin boards. You can refer to the on-line index for a list of conference subjects. In order to participate in a particular discussion, you have to "join" that conference. Then you can read and reply to messages that interest you.

## Using Data Libraries

The Source offers many programs that you may want to acquire. Some of these are in compressed format to speed up their transmission, and they must be expanded, or *unpacked*, before you can use them. First, we'll review the basic procedure for receiving files, and then we'll discuss how to unpack the ones in compressed format.

**Receiving Files**    As an example, suppose that you wanted a file called SDIR51.ARC, which is a utility program for sorting directories and other related tasks. You would use the following procedure to receive it:

1. After you log onto The Source, you will be presented with the entry menu, as shown in Figure 16.2.

2. From the entry menu, you can access the service that you want to use either by going through the menu system (press 2 to select the Menu of Services option) or directly by pressing Q for Quit and typing the name of the service. Figure 16.3 shows the menu displayed when you choose the Menu of Services option. For this example, however, press Q to enter the service directly.

3. When you see the − > prompt, type

    IBMSIG

    This displays the IBMSIG Main menu. Figure 16.4 shows a sample of that menu.

**Figure 16.2:**

*The Source's
Entry menu.*

```
    IBMSIG Main Menu <IBMSIG>

        October 28, 1986

        Welcome MKT027!

(* indicates special, low SIG rates.)     Updated:

    1  * PC User's Databases
    2  * IBMSIG Post Bulletins
    3  * IBMSIG Members Directory
    4    IBM Conferences (PARTI)
    5  * IBMSIG Library of Files/Programs
    6  * Program/System Request
    7    SourceMail
    8  * Products/Services
    9  * IBMSIG General Information          3 Jun 1986

Enter item number, <Q>uit or <H>elp: _



 Esc for ATtention, Home to SWitch      Capture Off     On: 00:06:19
```

**Figure 16.3:**

*The Source's
Services
menu.*

```
MENU OF SERVICES <MENU>

    1  Today From The Source <TODAY>
    2  News, Weather and Sports <NEWS>
    3  Business and Investing <BUSINESS>
    4  Communication Services <COMM>
    5  Special Interest Groups <SIGS>
    6  Personal Computing <PC>
    7  Travel Services <TRAVEL>
    8  Education, Shopping and Games <HOME>
    9  Member Information <INFO> **FREE**

Enter item number, <H>elp or <Q>uit: _






 Esc for ATtention, Home to SWitch      Capture Off     On: 00:09:24
```

**Figure 16.4:**

*The IBMSIG Main menu.*

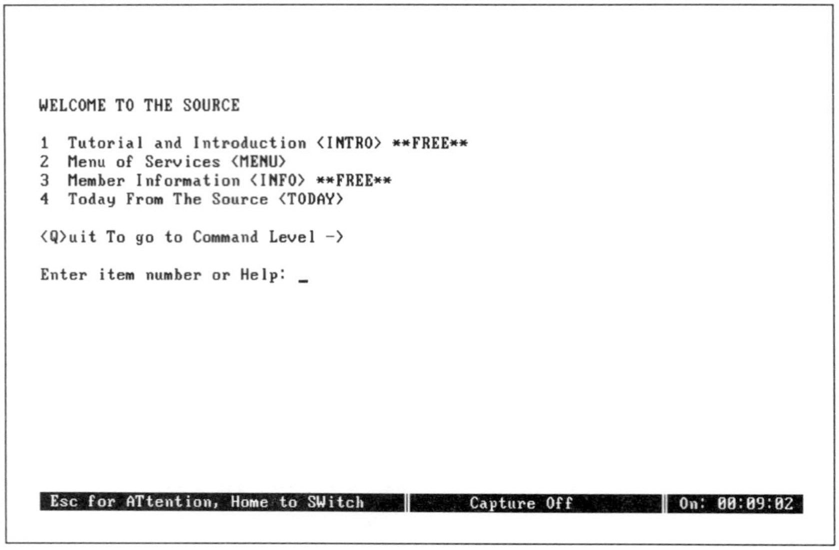

```
WELCOME TO THE SOURCE

1  Tutorial and Introduction <INTRO> **FREE**
2  Menu of Services <MENU>
3  Member Information <INFO> **FREE**
4  Today From The Source <TODAY>

<Q>uit To go to Command Level ->

Enter item number or Help: _




    Esc for ATtention, Home to SWitch        Capture Off        On: 00:09:02
```

4.  Press 5 to choose the IBMSIG Library of Files/Programs option from the menu. Figure 16.5 shows the menu that you will see now.

5.  Press 1 to select the Search Library of Files/Programs option. You will see the list of options shown in Figure 16.6. You can search for a file by reference to a keyword, date, user, or file name. You can also scan all the files.

6.  Press K to search by keywords.

7.  Enter the keyword

    DIRECTORY

    The Source will report the number of items found for that keyword.

8.  Press N to narrow down the search.

9.  Press K to narrow it down by keywords.

10. Enter the keyword

    SORT

    Again, The Source will report the number of items

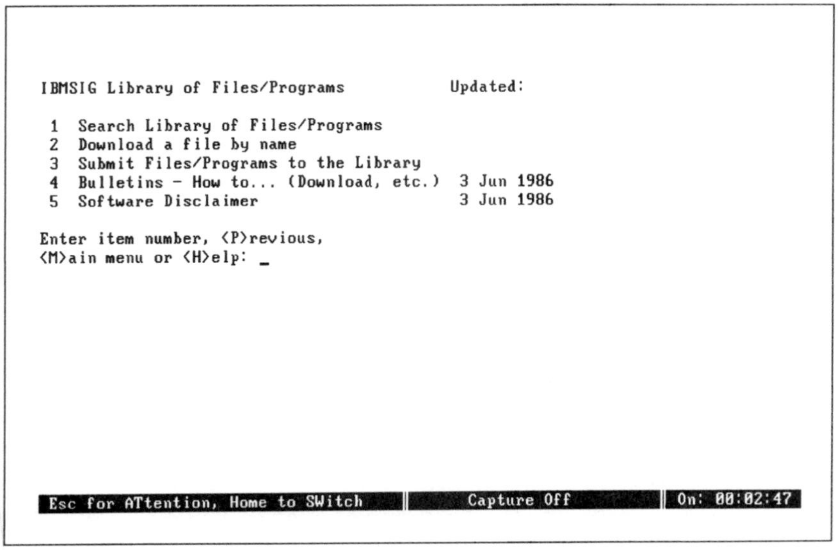

**Figure 16.5:**

*IBMSIG
Library of
Files/
Programs
menu.*

```
IBMSIG Library of Files/Programs         Updated:

  1  Search Library of Files/Programs
  2  Download a file by name
  3  Submit Files/Programs to the Library
  4  Bulletins - How to... (Download, etc.)  3 Jun 1986
  5  Software Disclaimer                      3 Jun 1986

Enter item number, <P>revious,
<M>ain menu or <H>elp: _




 Esc for ATtention, Home to SWitch      Capture Off      On: 00:02:47
```

found. Figure 16.6 shows the list of options with the entries for our sample search.

11. Now that the list of matching files is small enough, type

    SC

    to scan through them. You will see a display like the one shown in Figure 16.7.

12. Because SDIR51.ARC is a binary-data file, you must use the Kermit protocol to receive it. Enter

    KE

13. Press 2 to select the file.

14. Press Return to tell The Source that you are ready to receive the file.

15. Press Esc to put Crosstalk into command mode.

16. Enter

    RKERMIT

    This tells Crosstalk to receive a file using the Kermit

**Figure 16.6:**

*Searching for a file on The Source.*

```
Select by
<K>eyword, <D>ate, <U>ser id,
<FI>le name or <ALL>: K

Enter Keyword: DIRECTORY

43 item(s) found for
KEYWORDS = DIRECTORY

<N>arrow <E>xpand <REC>ap
<R>ead <SC>an <C>ancel: N

Narrow by
<K>eyword, <D>ate, <U>ser id,
<FI>le name or <ALL>: K

Enter Keyword: SORT

12 item(s) found when narrowed by
KEYWORDS = SORT

<N>arrow <E>xpand <REC>ap
<R>ead <SC>an <C>ancel: _
Esc for ATtention, Home to SWitch        Capture Off          On: 00:05:29
```

**Figure 16.7:**

*A sample list of files displayed by The Source.*

```
Screen 1

  1    ffm.arc           SIG003   8 Sep 1986   0:00   18534
       DUAL DIRECTORY LIST SORT MARK COPY DELETE BACKUP SUBDIRECTORY

  2    sdir51.arc        SIG004  31 Jul 1986   0:00   10240
       DOS SORTED DIRECTORY 5.1 EXECUTE COMMANDS PROGRAMS SORT UTILITY

  3    wd.arc            SIG004   3 Jul 1986   0:00   18176
       DOS SORTED DIRECTORY COLOR FILES SIZES SPACE OPTIONS UTILITY

  4    tf.arc            SIG004   4 Jun 1986   0:00   38912
       TURBO PASCAL TELEPHONE DIRECTORY SORT FIND LIST PRINT UTILITY

  5    dtk.arc           BCJ386  17 May 1986   0:00   52795
       DIRECTORY TOOL KIT BASIC RUN ATTRIBUTE DATE TIME SORT LABEL VOLUME

* - indicates item is a package

Enter item number(s) for description,
<KE>rmit, <XM>odem or <DI>splay to download a file,
<SC>an package contents, or <H>elp: _
Esc for ATtention, Home to SWitch        Capture Off          On: 00:04:52
```

protocol. Note that you do not have to tell Crosstalk the file name because The Source will send it.

17. Press Return to tell The Source to start sending the file. You will see Crosstalk's summary of the file transfer while it is in progress, and The Source will tell you when the transfer is complete.

The procedure for receiving text files in ASCII form is essentially the same, except that you do not have to use the Kermit protocol. Instead of entering KE (step 12 above), you would type

DI

To tell Crosstalk that you're going to receive a file (step 16 above), enter the CAPTURE command followed by the file name. For example, to receive a file named NEWS.TXT, type

CAPTURE NEWS.TXT

**Unpacking Compressed Files** Files with the extension .ARC are in a compressed form and must be unpacked before you can use them. If you do not have a utility program that does this, you can get one from The Source. At the time of writing, the file ARC51.COM is available on The Source in IBMSIG, and you can receive it by using the procedure outlined above. When you run ARC51.COM on your PC, it will unpack itself into a program file and documentation files. The program file is ARC.COM, and you can use that to unpack the SDIR51.ARC file and any other .ARC files that you receive from The Source. Incidentally, it also works with .ARC files offered on CompuServe.

The ARC.COM program also enables you to create compressed files with the extension .ARC yourself. You can use it to compress or decompress files that you are transmitting to The Source, to business colleagues, or to friends. The program will take quite a long time to receive, but should be worth the time involved because it will give you access to a large number of .ARC files. If you only want the unpacking utility, and do not want to create your own .ARC files, you can use one of the other utility programs available on The Source. You can find them by searching under the keyword ARCHIVE.

## Getting a Stock Quote

One of The Source's investment services is quoting stock prices. You can register a list of the stocks in your portfolio and see how all of them are doing, or you can obtain a quote for an individual stock.

Figure 16.8 shows a script file that obtains a quote for a stock and saves it in a file.

If you want to use this script file, first type it in and save it as SQUOTE.XTS. Then log onto The Source, and from any prompt, press Esc to put Crosstalk in command mode. To run the program, enter

DO SQUOTE

Crosstalk will ask you for the stock symbol (e.g., IBM) and a file name, then ask you to press Y to confirm. If you press another key, the file will jump to the EXIT section. If

**Figure 16.8:**

*A script file for obtaining a stock quote from The Source.*

```
; First ask for company symbol
ASK @S1 Give the company symbol _

; Ask for the file name
ASK @S5 Give the name of the file to save the data in _

; Get confirmation
ASK Press 'Y' to confirm _
IF -Y JUMP EXIT

; Check source mode

ASK Press 'Y' if you are in command mode (the -> prompt is shown)
IF Y JUMP OK

REPLY Q|
WAIT For '>'

LABEL OK

CAPTURE @S5
REPLY INVEST 1|

WAIT String "Select"
REPLY SY|

WAIT String "Symbol"
REPLY @S1|

WAIT Delay 20
CAPTURE OFF

REPLY Q|

LABEL EXIT
MESSAGE
Finished
.
```

you do press Y, it will ask you whether you are in command mode. You are in The Source's command mode if the – > prompt is on the screen. Type Y if you have this prompt. If you are not in The Source's command mode, Crosstalk will send the command Q followed by a carriage return to place you there.

Crosstalk will then go to the stock quote service, select the Access by Symbol option, send the symbol of the stock that you are interested in, wait for the quote, and return you to command mode on The Source. To repeat the procedure for another stock, all you need to do is enter

DO

## Logging Off

The Source's command to log off is

LOG

After you enter this command, The Source will return you to the network. From there, you will have to disconnect the line yourself by using Crosstalk's BYE command.

# 17
# Using Crosstalk
# with Dow Jones
# News/Retrieval

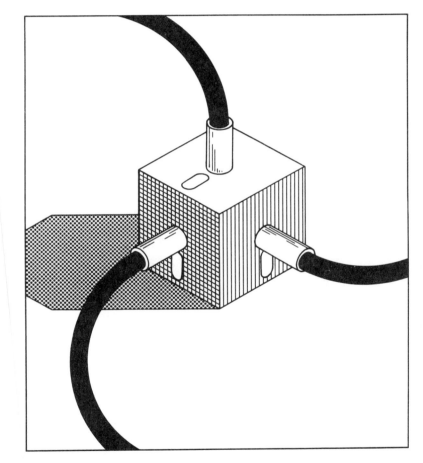

Dow Jones News/Retrieval (DJNR) is an on-line information service provided by Dow Jones & Co., Inc. It offers access to news, current and historical stock quotes, weather reports, and corporate information. DJNR also provides access to some commercial services that are available elsewhere, such as the Official Airline Guide, MCI Mail, and the Academic American Encyclopedia.

## Accessing DJNR

You can access DJNR through Tymnet, Telenet, Uninet or, in Canada, Datapac. The sample command file below can be used to dial the service through either Tymnet or Telenet.

For both networks, you should set 8 data bits, no parity, 1 stop bit, and full duplex. You can adapt the following command file for your own use, as explained in the second column.

| | |
|---|---|
| NUMBER 123-1234 | Insert the local access number for Tymnet or Telenet. |
| DATA 8 | Set 8 data bits. |
| SPEED 1200 | Set a baud rate of 300 or 1,200. |
| STOP 1 | Set 1 stop bit. |
| PARITY NONE | Set no parity. |
| DUPLEX FULL | Set full duplex. |
| GO | |

## Logging On

As with the log-on script files for CompuServe and The Source, the contents of your script file for logging onto DJNR depend on which network you are using. Examples of script files for logging on through Tymnet and Telenet are shown in Figures 17.1 and 17.2, respectively.

The Tymnet script file is the simpler of the two. It is a series of alternating WAIT and REPLY commands. The file

**Figure 17.1:**

*A log-on script file for accessing DJNR through Tymnet.*

```
; DJNR.XTS - TYMNET Version

WAIT Quiet 40
REPLY A
WAIT String "LOG IN"
REPLY DOW1;;
WAIT String "SERVICE"
REPLY DJNR|
WAIT String "PASSWORD"
REPLY SECRET|
```

**Figure 17.2:**

*A log-on script file for accessing DJNR through Telenet.*

```
; DJNR.XTS - TELENET Version

WAIT Quiet 20
REPLY |
REPLY |
WAIT String "TERMINAL"
REPLY D1|
WAIT F@
REPLY C 60942|
WAIT String "CONNECTED"
WAIT String "PLEASE"
REPLY DJNS|
WAIT String "@@@@@@@@"
REPLY SECRET|
REPLY |
```

begins by waiting for 4 seconds of silence, and then replies A. When it receives the string *LOG IN*, it replies DOW1;;. The next string it waits for is *SERVICE*, and to this it replies DJNR carriage return. The last string the file waits for is PASSWORD. Substitute your own DJNR password for the reply of SECRET.

The Telenet script file begins by waiting for 2 seconds of silence, and then gives two successive replies of a carriage return. It waits for the string *TERMINAL* and replies D1 carriage return; waits for an at sign (@) and replies C 60942 carriage return; then waits for a string of *CONNECTED* followed by a string of *PLEASE* and replies DJNS carriage return. Finally, the file waits for a string of eight at signs and replies SECRET carriage return and ends with another carriage return reply. As in the Tymnet script file, replace the reply of SECRET with your own DJNR password.

## Current Quotes

One of the most popular services provided by DJNR is the Current Quotes facility, which displays the current prices of quoted stocks. To use this facility, enter

//CQ

Then enter the abbreviation for the stock. You can specify up to five separate stocks in a single request. For example, to obtain quotes for IBM and Xerox, you would enter

IBM XRX

DJNR will then display the close and open, high and low, and last prices, and the volume traded. Figure 17.3 shows a sample screen displaying the current quotes for IBM and Xerox stocks.

If you check the prices of the same stocks frequently, you can use a script file to reduce the length of time that you are connected to DJNR. As an example, Figure 17.4 shows a script file that checks the prices of IBM and Xerox for you, captures the results to a file, and logs off. I've named the sample file QUOTES.XTS.

To run the sample script file, first log onto DJNR, press Esc to enter Crosstalk's command mode, and then enter

DO QUOTES

Crosstalk will take over from there and record the information for you.

**Figure 17.3:**

*A sample screen displayed by the DJNR Current Quotes facility.*

```
//CQ

CURRENT DAY QUOTES  BEING ACCESSED

ENTER QUERY
   IBM XRX


DOW JONES STOCK QUOTE REPORTER SERVICE
STOCK QUOTES DELAYED OVER 15 MINUTES
*=CLOSE PRICE ADJUSTED FOR EX-DIVIDEND


STOCK      BID      ASKED
           CLOSE    OPEN    HIGH     LOW       LAST     VOL(100'S)
IBM        121 1/8  120 3/4 122 1/8  120 1/2   121 7/8  14378
XRX        54 7/8   54 5/8  55       54 1/4    54 7/8   2392
-




 Esc for ATtention, Home to SWitch       Capture Off        On: 00:01:12
```

You could make the process even simpler by adding the commands in the script file shown in Figure 17.4 to the end of your log-on script file. That way, you could obtain the quotes by simply invoking Crosstalk with the name of the DJNR command file (assuming your log-on script file has the same name). For example, if your command file is DJNR.XTK and your script file is DJNR.XTS, you would enter

    XTALK DJNR

and Crosstalk would dial DJNR, log on, request the quotes, save the results in a file, and log off—all automatically.

## Weather Reports

DJNR also provides weather reports. You can obtain detailed information about the weather in all parts of the United States, as well as a summary of weather in other countries.

As an example, here's how you would view the three-day forecast for Providence, Rhode Island.

1. Enter the Weather Report section by typing

       //WTHR

   This displays the main menu for this section. Figure 17.5 shows a sample of the screen displayed.

2. Press N to display the menu shown in Figure 17.6.

3. From this menu, press 2 to select the Northeastern Cities option. DJNR displays the weather report in

**Figure 17.4:**

*A script file for obtaining quotes for IBM and Xerox.*

```
; QUOTES.XTS

REPLY //CQ|
WAIT String "QUERY"
CA QUOTE
REPLY IBM XRX|
WAIT Quiet 40
CA -
REPLY DISC|
WAIT Quiet 30
BYE
```

**Figure 17.5:**

*A DJNR
Weather
Report menu.*

```
//WTHR
DOW JONES NEWS/RETRIEVAL WEATHER REPORT
   COPYRIGHT (C) 1986 ACCU-WEATHER INC.
             ALL RIGHTS RESERVED.
PRESS FOR
1  Friday's Forecast: Rain Coming
        To West; Snow In Mountains
2  Early Season Blizzard Recalled -
        At Least In South Dakota
3  Weather Guide: Detailed Forecasts
        For Major Metropolitan Areas
4  The Outlook: Slow-Moving System
        Bringing Wet Weather To West

-------------------------------------------
PRESS FOR 3-DAY FORECASTS FOR U.S.
CITIES OR F FOR FOREIGN WEATHER TABLES.
-




       Esc for ATtention, Home to SWitch          Capture Off          On: 00:01:59
```

**Figure 17.6:**

*The DJNR
National
Weather
menu.*

```
N
10/17/86                   PAGE 1 OF 2
            NATIONAL WEATHER
PRESS FOR

  1    Key To Abbreviations
          Used In 3-Day Forecast Tables
  2    Northeastern Cities

  3    Middle Atlantic Cities

  4    South Central Cities

  5    Southeastern Cities
  -

                    .




       Esc for ATtention, Home to SWitch          Capture Off          On: 00:02:34
```

two pages. An example of the first page is shown in Figure 17.7.

4. Press Return to view the second page. Figure 17.8 shows a sample of the second page, which lists the forecasts for Providence.

If you use DJNR's weather report service to obtain information about the same regions frequently, you can write a script file for this purpose. Figure 17.9 shows the script file that automates the example described above. As with the commands in the script file for obtaining stock quotes, you could add the contents of the weather report script file to the end of your log-on script file to automate further the procedure.

Unlike most computer systems, DJNR does not have a regular prompt character or message; it just sits and waits for you to press a key. This makes programming script files for DJNR somewhat more complicated. One way to deal with this problem is to have Crosstalk wait for a certain period of silence rather than for a character or string. In the sample script file in Figure 17.9, after the first page is

**Figure 17.7:**

*A sample DJNR weather report for Northeastern cities, page 1 of 2.*

```
2
WEATHER 10/17/86          PAGE  1 OF  2

    Northeastern Cities

            ---
            FRI     SAT     SUN
    Albany   49/32sh 51/29s  49/36pc
    Atln Cty 56/40c  56/40pc 56/40pc
    Boston   55/36pc 46/34c  46/29s
    Burlingtn 44/27sf 45/29c 49/30pc
    Buffalo  47/33c  49/33s  53/36pc
    Chrlston 62/40c  62/42s  60/45pc
    Hartford 54/32pc 48/31c  48/30s
    New York 58/40c  52/38pc 53/38pc
    Philadel 56/42c  56/40pc 58/42pc
    Pttsburgh 52/37c 54/32s  57/38pc

    -

    Esc for ATtention, Home to SWitch    Capture Off    On: 00:03:05
```

**Figure 17.8:**

*A sample DJNR weather report for Northeastern cities, page 2 of 2.*

```
WEATHER 10/17/86          PAGE  2 OF  2

                  FRI      SAT      SUN
      Provdence 56/34pc  49/32c   49/32s
      Springfld 52/31pc  47/29c   46/30s
      Syracuse  48/33c   51/33s   50/36pc
   _



   ┌──────────────────────────────┐ ┌──────────────┐ ┌──────────────┐
    Esc for ATtention, Home to SWitch    Capture Off       On: 00:04:24
```

**Figure 17.9:**

*A sample script file for obtaining a DJNR weather report.*

```
; WEATHER.XTS

REPLY //WTHR|
WAIT String "TABLES"
CA WEATHER.REP
REPLY N|
WAIT String "5"
REPLY 2|
WAIT Quiet 30
REPLY |
WAIT Quiet 30
CA -
REPLY DISC|
WAIT Quiet 20
BYE
WAIT Quiet 20
QU
```

displayed, I've included the line

    WAIT Quiet 30

This asks Crosstalk to wait for 3 seconds of silence, which is the only way that it can detect the end of the first page of data.

## Other DJNR Information

DJNR contains many other databases, including those that provide current news, articles from the Wall Street Journal, and historical stock quotes. Obtaining information from on-line databases tends to be a very interactive process; you gradually narrow down your search by asking a series of questions. Thus, Crosstalk's script file facilities are not very helpful unless you always search for the exact same information. However, Crosstalk's SNAPSHOT and CAPTURE commands are very useful for searching databases. You can save time by capturing the text or screen while you're on-line and reviewing the data later.

## Logging Off

DJNR's command to log off is

DISC

After you enter this command, DJNR will return you to the network. From there, you will have to disconnect the line yourself by using Crosstalk's BYE command.

# Glossary

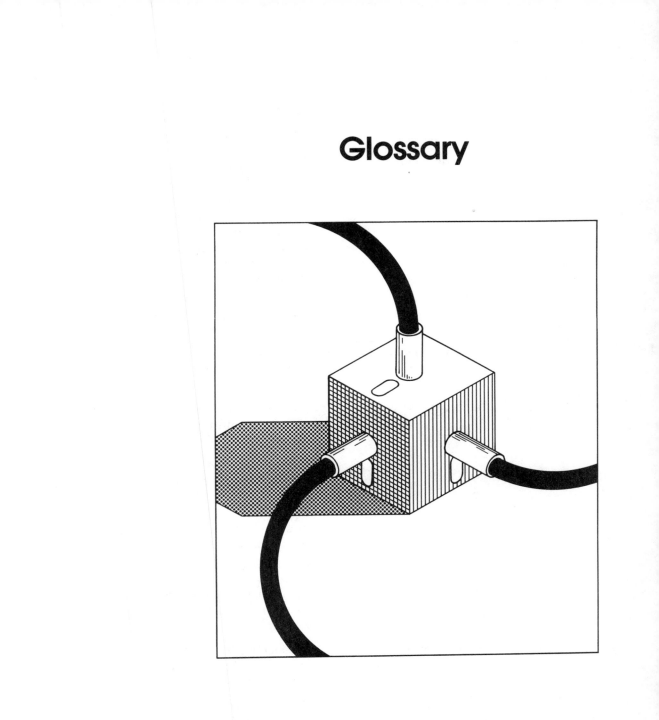

| | |
|---|---|
| ACK | Acknowledge, ASCII code 6. Used to acknowledge receipt of a transmission. |
| acoustic coupler | A modem attached to the handset of a telephone. |
| ASCII | American Standard Code for Information Interchange. A set of numbers from 0 through 127 assigned to letters, numerals, punctuation marks, and special characters. |
| asynchronous | Methods of communication in which the intervals between characters can be of uneven length. |
| Attention key | Key used to enter Crosstalk's command mode. Normally the Esc key. |
| baud rate | The length of the shortest signalling condition or event, divided into 1 second. |
| bit | Binary digit. A number which can only have the value of 1 or 0. |
| block | The same as a *packet*. |
| break | A special signal used to interrupt a program. |
| Break key | Key used to transmit a *break*. |
| buffer | An area of memory containing data to be transmitted or processed. |
| bulletin board | An electronic database holding messages which can be read and received by a number of users. |
| bps | Bits per second. The number of binary digits of information transmitted in 1 second. |

| | |
|---|---|
| capture | To copy incoming data to memory or to disk. |
| capture buffer | Area of memory in which received data are stored. |
| CD | The carrier detect line. Used by a modem to indicate presence of a carrier signal. Line 8 on RS-232 connections. |
| COM1, COM2 | Names given by PC-DOS and MS-DOS to refer to the serial ports on an IBM PC or compatible computer. |
| command file | A file containing a list of Crosstalk commands and parameters, having the extension .XTK. |
| command line | The line appearing at the bottom of the screen when Crosstalk is in *command mode,* and where commands entered by the user are displayed as they are typed. |
| command mode | The state of Crosstalk in which keystrokes typed by the user are interpreted as commands to Crosstalk rather than as characters to be transmitted. |
| computer conferencing | A facility whereby several users discuss a topic by sending messages to a central computer. |
| D-type connector | The most common connector for connecting cables to serial devices, normally having either 25 or 9 pins (male connectors) or sockets (female connectors). |
| data bits | The bits forming part of a single group of bits that represent data, as opposed to start, parity, and stop bits. |

DCE

Data communication equipment. Modems and other intermediate communications devices (distinguished from *DTE*).

display window

The area of the *status screen* used for displaying data to the user.

Dow Jones News/Retrieval

An on-line service offering news, current and historic stock information, and other information services.

download

To cause a file of data to be transmitted by a remote computer and saved locally.

DSR

The data set ready line. The primary handshaking line from DCE to DTE. Line 6 in RS-232 connections.

DTE

Data terminal equipment. Terminals and other devices that are the source or final destination of data.

DTR

The data terminal ready line. The primary handshaking line from DTE to DCE. Line 20 in RS-232 connections.

ENQ/ACK

A handshaking protocol using the ENQ, ACK, and NAK characters.

escape sequence

A sequence of characters, normally starting with the Escape character, that has a special meaning to a terminal, such as a command to clear the screen.

even parity

Adding a bit after the data bits to make the total number of binary ones in the bits an even number.

flow control

In communications, methods whereby a receiving device can control the flow of data from a transmitting device. In programming, methods whereby the commands in a program can be executed other than sequentially.

full-screen processing

Methods whereby a terminal can be made to display characters at any position on the screen.

glass TTY

A terminal emulating a Teletype printer.

handshaking

Methods whereby a receiving device can control the flow of data from a transmitting device.

hardware interrupt

A signal sent from a device indicating the occurrence of an event.

IRQ

An interrupt request line. A circuit used to transmit a signal when a specified event occurs.

Kermit

A protocol designed for microcomputer to mainframe file transfers.

LAN

Local area network. A system connecting a number of communications devices in one location.

modem

*Mod*ulator *dem*odulator. A device for converting computer communications to and from a form appropriate to the telephone network.

network

A system connecting a number

of communications devices.

| | |
|---|---|
| no parity | The omission of a parity bit. |
| node | A part of a network having a number of circuits connected to it which are consolidated for onward transmission. |
| null modem | A set of circuits that enables two DTE or two DCE devices to be connected by swapping the necessary wires. |
| odd parity | Adding a bit after the data bits to make the total number of binary ones in the bits an odd number. |
| packet | A group of data elements transmitted together, generally forming part of a larger transmission comprising a number of packets. A packet includes additional information, such as the packet number and error-detecting codes. |
| packet switching | A method of communication involving splitting a transmission up into packets. Successive packets along a given channel can belong to different transmissions. |
| parity bit | A bit sent after the data bits, used for error detection. It is computed from the data bits by both the transmitting and receiving devices, and the result is then compared. |
| parity error | The condition arising when the parity bit is not correctly related to the data bits. |
| protocol | A set of standards covering data communications. |

RI

Ring indicator line. Used by a modem to indicate that it is receiving a call and would be ringing if it were a telephone. Line 22 in RS-232 connections.

RQS or RTS

Request to send line. Secondary handshaking line from DTE to DCE. Line 4 in RS-232 connections.

RXD

Received data line. The circuit carrying data from DCE to DTE. Line 3 in RS-232 connections.

script file

A file containing a list of commands to Crosstalk that automate a communications session.

serial communications

The transmission of data as a sequence of bits.

serial interface

A circuit enabling a device to transmit and/or receive data as a sequence of bits.

SG

Signal ground line. A common reference point for various circuits. Line 7 in RS-232 connections.

snapshot buffer

An area of memory in which Crosstalk saves an image of the screen for later review.

start bit

A bit sent in *asynchronous* communications indicating the start of a new character.

status line

The bottom line of the screen when a communications session is in progress and Crosstalk is not in *command mode*.

stop bit

A bit sent in *asynchronous* communications indicating the end of a character.

Switch key

The key used to switch between the terminal screen and the status screen. Normally the Home key.

synchronous communications

The transmission of a sequence of data elements at regularly spaced intervals without the use of start and stop bits to frame each character.

Telenet

A commercial packet-switching network.

terminal emulation

Methods whereby a computer can be made to act as a terminal.

terminal screen

The screen normally displayed by Crosstalk while a communications session is in progress.

timeout

A period after which if no response is received, an error is considered to have occurred.

true compatible

A microcomputer that runs all software intended for the IBM PC.

TXD

Transmitted data line. The line carrying data from DTE to DCE. Line 2 in RS-232 connections.

upload

To transmit a file to a remote computer.

unpack

To cause a compressed file to be expanded to its original format.

XMODEM

A protocol designed for transfers between microcomputers.

word length

The number of data bits sent at one time during *asynchronous* communications.

# Index